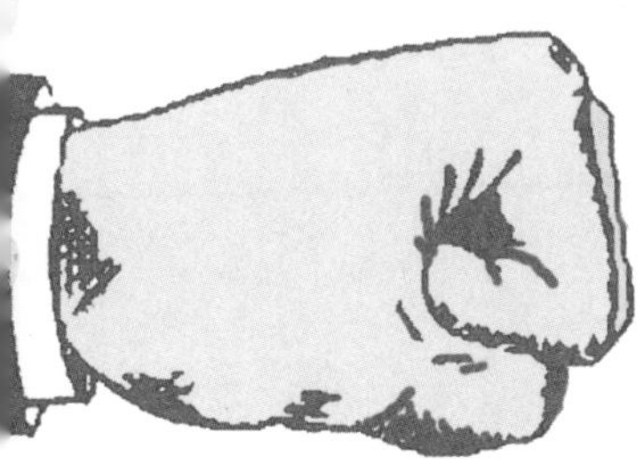

THINGS I WANT TO PUNCH IN THE FACE

THINGS I WANT TO PUNCH IN THE FACE

JENNIFER WORICK

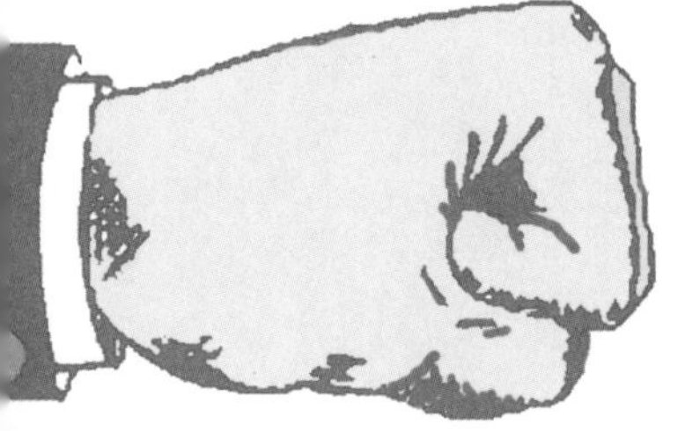

The views expressed in this book are solely those of the author, and she means no harm by them. Unless you decide to sue her, in which case she'll want to punch you in the face.

Published by Prospect Park Media
969 S. Raymond Avenue
Pasadena, California 91105
prospectparkmedia.com

Library of Congress Cataloging-in-Publication Data

Worick, Jennifer.
Things I want to punch in the face / by Jennifer Worick. — 1st ed.
p. cm.
ISBN 978-0-9834594-7-7
1. American wit and humor. I. Title.
PN6165.W66 2012
973.9202'07--dc23
2012013640

ISBN: 978-0-9834594-7-7

First edition, first printing

DESIGNED BY KATHY KIKKERT.

Manufactured in the United States of America.

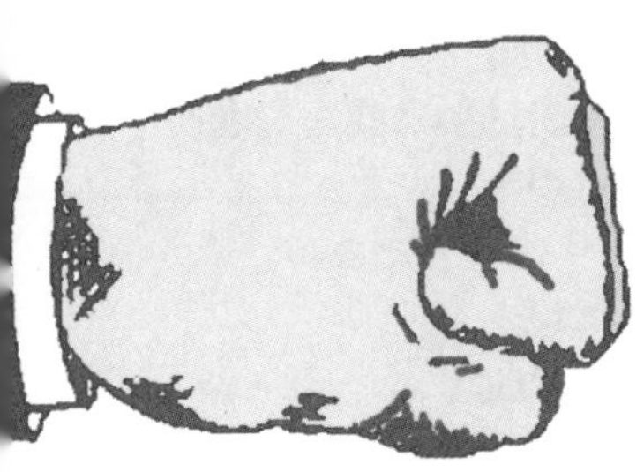

THINGS I WANT TO PUNCH IN THE FACE

THE TABLE

OF PUNCHES

Naked Pregnancy Portraits
Namaste
Navel Lint
New Year's Eve
New Yorker Cartoons
Non-prescription Eyeglasses
Old-guy Facelifts
Old-guy Ponytails
Pajamas as Outerwear
Parents Who Give Their
 Offspring Names Starting
 with the Same Letter
Parking Hogs
Patchouli
Peach Schnapps
Penis Names
People Who Blab on Red-eyes
People Who Don't Believe in TV
People Who Stop at the
 Top of Escalators
People Who Watch All the Credits
Petting Zoos
Pollen
Precious Moments
Prolific Dead People
Quadraboob & Uniboob
Renaissance Faires
Scrabble
Seat Hogs
Shoeless Households
Sidewalk Hogs
Silk Flowers
SkyMall
Spinning Beach Ball
Staycations
Steampunk
Stripper Brows
Sunglasses at Night
Talking About Yourself
 in the Third Person
Tennis Bracelets
Topping Off Coffee Without Asking
Twenty-minute Coffee Prep
TYPING E-MAILS IN ALL CAPS
Utilikilts
Vanity Plates
Ventriloquists' Dummies
White Chocolate
Windsocks
Winks
Xtina
Year-Round Christmas Decorations
Zumba

and finally...
Books Derived from Blogs

INTRODUCTION

Welcome to *Things I Want to Punch in the Face,* a non-rose-colored-glasses view on life. See, things irk my shit on a daily basis. Alone, they are not a big deal, but add to it a stressed gal with a short fuse and you get—you guessed it, Einstein!—something I want to punch in the face.

So without further ado, I present my take-no-prisoners take on life's little annoyances.

For instance, I'd like to smack down waiters who top off my coffee without asking. I might have just gotten it to the right temperature and blend of cream and sugar when they come along and fill up my decaf cup with regular joe while I'm eyeballing the dessert menu. I'm the boss of me, not someone with a nametag! I want to punch these presumptive knobs in the face.

I'm not gonna lie: This isn't a new phenomenon. It's easy to say that I'm as bitter as black coffee because of the economy or my perpetually single status or an extra ten pounds. I could talk about the crappy eight days that prompted me to actually start recording my peeves in ridiculous detail. But if I'm honest with myself, and with you, things bug me on a daily, if not hourly, basis. They always have. I'm generally a good-natured, dare I say happy, person, but I'm also human. Like Alanis Morissette, a fly in my Chardonnay isn't something I'm going to celebrate. (Unlike Alanis Morissette, I know the definition of "ironic.")

But I just might bitch about it, maybe even write about it. And I'm not alone. You probably have had moments or days where you wanted to kick something, scream, or burst out laughing at the absurdity of mimes or the SkyMall catalog. Maybe you even wanted to punch something in the face. Hard. Now's your chance, at least vicariously. And hey, if you really do have to clean something's clock, why not aim your fist at this book cover? I aim to please, and so I hope you'll be as pleased as punch reading these 102 entries as I was when I smacked them down.

GUIDE TO THE PUNCHES

ANNOYING

like a mild rash

AGGRAVATING

like a black eye

DISGUSTING

like an open sore

TOXIC

like acid reflux or IBS

PERMANENTLY DAMAGED

like my patience

AUTO-TUNE

PUNCH RATING 👊👊👊

I can't sing. I learned this a long time ago, when folks used to turn around and stare at me during Mass when I was trying to rock "Amazing Grace" or "Ave Maria." My tone-deafness was driven home during high school. Whenever the spring musical rolled around, I was relegated to the chorus or the comic relief cameo—both decidedly non-singing roles—and asked to mouth along to the group numbers.

I had my "come to Jesus" moment about my vocal chords long ago. God blessed me with so many other talents that it'd just be greedy to wish for the voice of Aretha Franklin. And we all know that greed is one of the Seven Deadly Sins.

> **FACT OF THE MATTER**
> ✦ **The path to musical hell is paved with good intentions—auto-tune was initially created by an Exxon engineer who was developing methods to interpret seismic data.**

I accept my shortcomings. So too should singalings like Rebecca Black (whose new heights of insipidity may be signaling the end of the world), Kim Zolciak, and Ke$ha, none of whom can carry a tune. And shame on folks like Usher, Cher, and wil.i.am, who actually can sing. Back away from the audio processor or I might have to auto-turn my fist toward your voicebox.

BACKHANDED COMPLIMENTS

PUNCH RATING

I can't get over how good you look.
You're so lucky. If I ate like you, I'd look like a house.
You don't look happy in that.
That sweater is...interesting.
I just think it's a little young for you.
It's a hat, all right!
You're more of a "street smart" kind of guy.
You're not the kind of girl guys date; you're the kind of girl they marry.
You're so evolved...for a man.

FACT OF THE MATTER
✦ There's a real name for this—asteism is a "genteel" way of deriding another. Here's my genteel response: Go away...please.

As a perfectly bred broad, let me be perfectly clear.

The backhanded compliment really should be called a backhanded cutdown, because there's absolutely nothing complimentary about these sort of comments. Worse than actual criticism, they drip with condescension, as though I am too thick to pick up on what you're really saying. Oh, I get it. And it sucks. You suck.

Spit it out and say what you mean, or keep your rude trap shut. If this dress makes my skin look like a rotten cantaloupe, I'd sorta like to know. If you think I said something inane, keep it to yourself. With loads of etiquette options in front of you, don't secretly delight in choosing the road less mannered. Don't rationalize away the passive-aggressive comment by believing you're refraining from saying what you really think. Instead of demonstrating tact, you're just putting the ass in class.

And in case that was unclear in any way, that's not a compliment.

BACK FAT

PUNCH RATING

It's bad enough that I have boobies busting out of my front side. Do I really need my body jutting out of my back? No matter my weight, when I strap on a bra, the layer of fat I've accumulated for winter hibernation oozes under and over the band.

Needless to say, this is decidedly not hot.

Don't misunderstand me: that layer of fat is insulating me, but it's the only thing keeping me warm, since no one wants to get near my built-in pillow. It's like spooning with Quasimodo. It's not all bad, I suppose. My punch-back is great for uncomfortable plane flights—no need to take up space in my carry-on with a bucky pillow when I'm rocking the Maidendeform.

FACT OF THE MATTER

A properly fitted bra can help minimize back fat. Going commando up top eliminates it altogether, although that typically brings issues of its own.

But that might be the only upside to my body goo. Oh, and I suppose there's one other consolation: if I punch back fat in its face, it will absorb the impact and prevent any damage to my internal organs. There I go again, being all glass half-full and shit.

BAGGAGE CLAIM COCK BLOCK

PUNCH RATING 👊👊👊👊

Are you way more important than everyone else?
Is your luggage made of solid gold?
Are you smuggling someone across the border in a steamer trunk without air holes?
Did your water just break?

If you answered "yes" to any of these questions, fine. You might suck dead bear, but I'll give you a pass at the baggage claim carousel. If you answered "no," you must need me to fly my fist in a northerly direction toward your face.

Lemme tell you why.

When a flight lands, I try to hightail it out of the airport. Sometimes I'm forced to check a bag, so I haul ass from my arrival gate, only to find myself jockeying for position around the baggage carousel while I wait for my Samsonite to tumble down the conveyor belt. You'd think I'd be so flippin' happy to be off my flight and out of its Lilliputian seats that I'd just be content to feel my limbs again.

Uh, no.

The flightmare continues as I elbow my way through chuckleheads in pleated khakis or gamey business suits with phones clipped to their belts, parents who are wrangling several unruly kids hopped up on M&Ms, and reunited couples engaged in serious tonsil hockey. Who the fuck knows if my bag made it to my destination, since I can't see the conveyor belt, let alone get to it. Asshats of every kind queue up against the carousel, forming a Hands Across American Airlines bond that I can't break through. When a waste of space scores a bag, he doesn't remove it from the fray. No, he usually sets it beside himself to create an additional hurdle for me to trip over/kick the shit out of when I finally spy my bag amid the golf clubs, checked car seats, and floral tapestry suitcases littering the conveyor belt.

> **FACT OF THE MATTER**
> **In her song "Baggage Claim," Miranda Lambert is smart enough to avoid the baggage carousel, telling her kicked-to-the-curb lover, "When you hit the ground, check the lost and found, 'cuz it ain't my problem now."**

Then there are the families.

If you want to queue up like the von Trapp Family Singers, so be it. Just be aware that I'm going to use my carry-on bag and my laptop case to box your ears like a monkey rocking the cymbals. Find your roller bag now, bitch. I don't think that red ribbon you tied onto the handle is gonna help you.

BEACH MAKEUP & JEWELRY

PUNCH RATING

As the temperatures soar, I beeline to the beach. But instead of cooling off, my blood really starts to boil when I spot tantards tricked out in full-on makeup and their entire jewelry box. Even if you happen to be a Kardashian sister or are filming a reality show, back away from the waterproof eyeliner and the gold bangles.

Wearing the complete cosmetic cornucopia—foundation, blush, bronzer, eye shadow, eyeliner, mascara, lip liner, lipstick—is going to clog your pores, particularly if you add sunscreen into the mix. And when you wear a tangle of necklaces or a fistful of rings, you're adding tan lines, dulling your baubles, and risking their loss or damage.

> **FACT OF THE MATTER**
> **It's no small comfort to know that a bronzed babe's gold and silver will become tarnished when exposed to salt water.**

Oh, and you look fekking dumb. It's like you're trying too hard. Frankly, you look desperate. Sorry to put sand in your Spandex, but the beach is a place to chill and let your hair down. It's not the place to show off your new Shimmer Brick and tennis bracelet.

Step away from the MAC and the Maybelline, and leave the ghetto gold back at the beach house. Real beach bunnies have the confidence to embrace the elements and their natural beauty. I learned that from *Baywatch*.

BIZSPEAK

PUNCH RATING

Our business needs to grab the low-hanging fruit.

Take that idea offline and put it in the parking lot.

Let's have a meeting to drill down into that idea and then dogfood it to the company.

We need more bandwidth to support the hockey stick on the home page.

Schedule a meeting next week for a masterminding session on monetizing our site.

How can we get to yes?

> **FACT OF THE MATTER**
> **The Franklin Planner is named after Ben Franklin, who apparently had personal organization on his long list of accomplishments.**
>
> **FACT OF THE MATTER**
> **International Talk Like a Pirate (ITLAP) Day is September 19, matey.**

Um, are you developing a new language? You should know that the only cool language to invent is pirate speak, matey.

If you insist on talking nonsense in a bid to sound like you know what you're doing, I'm going to have to take out my Franklin Planner and beat you, restructuring content without boundaries from the top down. Oh, you want to brand yourself, you say? Pull down your flat-front trousers so I can go old-media on your ass and brand you with a red-hot poker.

This particular SOW is in my wheelhouse.

BLACK FRIDAY

PUNCH RATING 👊👊👊👊👊

I'm sure you'll agree with me that "Black Friday" evokes some sort of horrific tragedy, such as a massacre or a deadly plague or the end of days. And indeed, just for an extra 15 percent off, people risk exposure to H1N1 and women who will cut you with their coupon if given a chance.

> **FACT OF THE MATTER**
> **Our founding fathers would be so proud—the term "Black Friday" was coined around 1960 in that cradle of democrassy, Philadelphia.**

Am I the only one who thinks this scenario is absoloonly nuts?

This excruciating day has been called "Retail S&M." If I want a little slap and tickle, I sure as shit am not going to look for it in the aisles of Walmart on Whack Friday. God invented the internet so we can avoid hot strip-mall messes and crowded parking lots in favor of leftovers and online shopping.

BUCKET LISTS

PUNCH RATING 👊👊👊👊

I'm all for living your life to the fullest (like Bon Jovi says, "I just wanna live while I'm alive"), but there's something about putting your dreams and aspirations in a bucket that seems just plain wrong. Maybe if it was called the Silk Purse List or the Safety Deposit Box List or the Goody Drawer List, I could choke the idea down. But bucket? Can't we find a worthier receptacle for our unfulfilled desires?

I get it. Kick the bucket and all that. Riiiiight. When I'm in my death throes, am I expected to seize up and randomly punt a bucket that just happens to be sitting next to my deathbed? What, was I just digging up potatoes or mopping the floor? When I'm about to buy the farm, I don't envision myself as an indentured servant.

FACT OF THE MATTER

The film *The Bucket List* grossed upward of $175 million worldwide. On my bucket list? Punching director Rob Reiner in his meathead.

Fuck the bucket. Live each day like you are dying. Don't lie in bed, don't ask for ice chips, and don't check crap off a list. Go out, eat your way through all the lobster in Maine, have a lot of boom-chicka-boom-boom sex, be present in every single fucking moment, and lose the suck-it list. If you don't, I'll have no choice but to fulfill my lifelong dream of clocking you nine ways 'til Sunday. It's right up there with skydiving.

BURNING MAN

PUNCH RATING

Someone recently sent me a video of Burning Man revelers reciting *Oh, the Places You'll Go*.

It sent me to the medicine cabinet.

Just watching it gave me a sugar rush by way of heatstroke via straight-up migraine. But nothing can cure what ails me.

Lacking a peyote button or those handy *Hunger Games* suicide berries, I am forced to resort to writing as a way to alleviate my malady.

FACT OF THE MATTER

While you'd think Burning Man would have originated in the hippie dippy '60s, it actually began in 1986 as a Summer Solstice bonfire ritual on Baker Beach in San Francisco...which is pretty hippie fucking dippy.

Burning Man started in the mid-1980s as an artsy-fartsy homage to the Solstice, burning effigies as a form of "radical self-expression," clearly a hippie euphemism for a low-grade case of pyromania (and not the totally rad Def Leppard kind). I love fire like the Heat Miser, but this creeps me out. After sitting through the *Wicker Man* only to watch a dude burned alive as an offering for the harvest, I am not down with towering infernos.

Then there are the hipster hippies dropping acid while dropping trou. No. Just no. The Places I'll Go? Pretty sure my list doesn't include Black Rock City.

CARNATIONS

PUNCH RATING

My loathing of this wretched bloom probably started in high school, when cheerleaders would sell them as a fundraiser around Valentine's Day and Homecoming. The more flowers you received from cupids who could do the splits, the more popular you clearly were. And the popular bitches would carry those stinky stalks around from class to class.

Let's just say, I did not have a bouquet stuck out of my Trapper Keeper.

Nowadays, I hate the crapass carnation for all new reasons. It stinks. You can often buy the dyed blue variety at gas stations. Classy. It fills in for better buds at funeral homes and the racetrack. As a boutonnière, it becomes a ball of blech.

Carnations are supposed to represent fascination and distinction. They can have the distinction of being the first flower to fascinate at my incoming fist. The time is nigh to mulch these asshole flowers into a pulp. And after putting the petal to the metal of my rototiller, I am happy to report that I now only smell success.

Baby's breath, you're on notice. If you know what's good for you, you'll steer clear.

FACT OF THE MATTER

✦ As if January babies weren't hosed enough already, coming after the gift-giving extravaganza of December, they have to put up with the carnation as their birth flower.

CELEBRITY BABY NAMES

PUNCH RATING

Pop quiz: Which of these are actual Hollywood baby names?
a. Ikhyd
b. Reign Beau
c. Audio Science
d. Pilot Inspektor
e. All of the above

You guessed it, being all smart and shit, that the answer is "All of the above."

I don't hate the players, I just hate the names. I'm happy to have these kids grow up and join my posse. Kal-El and Moxie Crimefighter can knock down my haters. Hermes is destined to be my personal shopper, and Reign Beau my nutritionist.

Kids have enough problems without insecure yet narcissistic parents saddling them with a nutbar name. Why not let them discover who they are, rather than assigning them a name that's sure to seal their fate? Ikhyd sounds like an exotic animal that can roam the plains alongside an okapi. Jermajesty and Banjo are gonna get their asses kicked up and down the playground. And even I feel fucked just thinking about Audio Science.

FACT OF THE MATTER

The name of Jason Lee's son, Pilot Inspektor, was inspired by the song "He's Simple, He's Dumb, He's the Pilot," by the band Grandaddy. I suppose it's better than the alternative of Simple Dumb Lee.

For shits and giggles, let's change your names and see how you like it. From here on out, Kal-El's daddy Nic Cage is going to be called

Lex Loser. Rachel Griffith (Banjo's mom) is hereby dubbed Accordion Fold. Ving Rhames sired Reign Beau, so I think it's more fitting to change his name to Pot O. Gold. Audio Science's mom, Shannyn Sossamon, can be tagged as "Exhibit A" and be used as a test subject in a research experiment.

And, finally, Robert Rodriguez, since you are a repeat offender (Rebel, Racer, Rocket, Rogue—ridiculous), I'm going to give you a special moniker; I'm thinking "Rectum" or "Reduce Reuse Recycle."

FACT OF THE MATTER

Barbara Hershey boarded the crazy train early on, naming her son Free in 1972. Clearly this came at a cost; Free changed his name to Tom when he was nine years old.

CELEBRITY FRAGRANCES

PUNCH RATING

Britney, Jessica, and Mariah keep churning out stinkers, and I'm not talking about their singles. Divas keep littering cosmetic counters with hiddy scents that are not "reminscent of classic Hollywood allure," like Forever Mariah Carey promises, but rather call to mind "poorly dressed skank" or "botched boob job."

When we whiff "Fantasy," are we supposed to forget about Britney's barefoot excursions to gas station bathrooms, let alone her cooch flashing, head-shaving, paparazzi-attacking antics? Are we supposed to experience a flight of "Fancy" when sniffing the treacly trifle that that arbiter of style Jessica Simpson approved between shopping at Fred Segal and getting a French mani?

FACT OF THE MATTER

The sweet smell of success: Perfume "makers" Avril Lavigne and Derek Jeter can thank Elizabeth Taylor for kickstarting the celeb fragrance movement; White Diamonds still stands as the best-selling celebrity fragrance in the United States.

I can smell the marketing bullshit from here, which I guarantee is celebrifree airspace. Even if a scent doesn't induce the gag reflex, do you really want a bottle of Fergie's Outspoken embarrassing your dressing table? Stop putting money in Kim Kardashian's low-rise jeans and Jessica Simpson's ginormous Louis Vuitton bag and just say no to eau de ho.

CHAI

PUNCH RATING 👊👊👊

Is it tea? Is it coffee? Is it just plain woo-woo pretentious? What the fuck are you, chai?

If you're not living in or touring India, chances are you are drinking a powdered version of this spiced milk tea, or even a bastardized chai/coffee hybrid. For instance, I just discovered to my dismay that a dirty chai doesn't involve extra olive juice, but a shot of espresso.

But it's not just the chai itself. It's the knobs who drink it. When sipping on this strange brew, these exotic creatures somehow feel enlightened and superior, much like I imagine Tom Cruise and his Scientology cronies feel after a good L. Ron Hubbard jamboree. Doctoring up their chai with a dollop of soy milk and a soupçon of cardamom, these wannabe Siddharthas eat, pray, and love throwing the stinkeye at my mocha choca latte and silently judging, all the while saying crap like "namaste, my friend" to my face while reaching for their heart center.

> **FACT OF THE MATTER**
> ✦ **Indian chai acts as a natural digestive.**
>
> **FACT OF THE MATTER**
> ✦ ***Chai* (or *cha*) is the generic word for tea in many countries.**

I want to punch these nirvana-in-a-cup-seeking sultans of swill in their third eye, until they're blind.

CHEETOS DUST

PUNCH RATING

Like Shakira's hips, Cheetos don't lie. When viewing the orange mist in my car, on my clothing, on my couch, it's clear that there's been a high Cheetos count lately. And if you were to turn on a black-light or spray some Luminol in my pad, you might see an occasional orange splatter pattern. Clearly, something really bad happened on the right side of my couch.

> **FACT OF THE MATTER**
> ✦ **Cheetos' flavor and composition can vary by geographic region. If you find yourself in Asia, sample Savory American Cream in China and Strawberry Cheetos in Japan.**

While I love to put away orangefood at every and any opportunity, I don't really like the radioactive goo that cakes my fingers. (Okay, that's a lie. I just hate the damage it does to my surroundings when I don't lick my fingers lickety split.) As I got out of the car recently, my pal gave me a strange look. She then attacked me, wiping me down and beating my clothes until a cloud of orange rose up around me. Thank God. Without her delousing, people on the street would have thought I had come out on the wrong side of a fight with a Tang canister.

I can't punch Cheetos in the face because it will only exacerbate the problem. The only thing to do is to throw some cold water on this all-unnatural snack food…literally. Either that, or I'm going to mix it with some lotion, create a faux-spray tan, and dress up as the entire Jersey Shore for Halloween—or an Oompa effing Loompa.

COMFORT SHOES

PUNCH RATING

We've put a man on the moon and created fabrics with UV protection. We've cloned a camel, for crying out loud. So I'm frankly puzzled as to why cushioned and supportive shoes invariably give you Frankenfeet. Bouncing along in personal flotation devices, you might feel fantastic, but you look like you've been in a car accident, what with those casts encasing your hooves and all.

Dansko, Birkenstock, Merrell, Easy Spirit, Earthies, and, ugh, Crocs—y'all are the red-headed stepchildren in my shoe wardrobe. You're part of the footwear family but should remain out of sight if you know what's good for you. Soles are bulbous, footbeds stanky, and uppers rounded, wide, and clunky. Sensible with a side of suck, these travesties manage to look like clown shoes while simultaneously announcing that you've just given up.

FACT OF THE MATTER

Birkenstock has a long-storied history shodding feet in the Vaterland; Johann Adam Birkenstock was registered way back in 1774 as a shoemaker. I hope someone smacked him in the face with a cork footbed.

If your designers can't cook up a sleek approach to comfort and cushioning soon, I'm going to dig out my red Dansko clogs and inflict a bit of blunt-force trauma. Did I just put my foot in your mouth?

COWLICKS

PUNCH RATING

I got my hair hacked off and I'm still wiggin' out, I'm not gonna lie. I spent enough time in the '80s trying to rock a "bi-level" 'do to know that cowlicks are not kind to short cuts (fifth grade is not kind to anyone).

My bangs are a constant challenge. The left side of my bangs, if left to its own devices, scrunches into a sort of zigzag pattern. Harry Potter may have his scar to bear, but I have a fucking lightning bolt lock of hair to suffer on a daily basis. And because I live in a rainy climate, this and other cowlicks roam free.

My brothers called me Heifer Head when I was a kid (Chris and John were real charmers), but now I suspect it's not because I was over my fighting weight. It's because my scalp was catnip to cows far and wide. Take the back of my head, for instance. Swirls and whorls give me a, um, fullness at my crown while pieces at my nape curve and peek out from the back of my neck, taunting me in the mirror with their everlasting defiance. Now that the back is shorn, I have a cockscomb of hair rising at the crown and fresh shoots sprouting from my nape.

FACT OF THE MATTER
The term "cowlick" dates from the 16th century, when Richard Haydocke coined the term. Thanks, Dickhead.

Fuck me.

My spirit is strong even if my follicles are weak, so I'm bringing out the styling paste and smothering, strangling, and smacking down those asshat cowlicks until they lie down and submit to my Bumble & Bumble.

Thank God I have a lot of hats.

CROSS-POLLINATED FOOD

PUNCH RATING

Some things, like peanut butter and chocolate or mac 'n cheese, are a match made in epicurean heaven. Then there's the cheeseburger pizza. Contrary to popular Pillsbury belief, it's not the best of both worlds. It's neither a cheeseburger nor a pizza. .

While I can tuck into a tater tot casserole like nobody's business, certain foods have no business commingling. Pick a lane, taco pie. Stop waffling, waffle sandwich. Pizza and lasagna are beautiful things on their own—why did Rachel Ray have to jump the shark with pizzagna? And McRib, you're just McWrong. Although I gotta hand it to McDonalds for having the 'nads to introduce a boneless, seemingly meatless McRib sandwich.

> **FACT OF THE MATTER**
> **Paula Deen's Lady Brunch Burger features a hamburger patty tarted up with a fried egg and bacon and bookended by two Krispy Kreme glazed doughnuts. Burgers and doughnuts are two foodstuffs that should never, ever meet on a plate.**

What's next? Chocolate chicken wings? A sausage-link latte? Tilapia crème brûlée? It's time to order up a large fist with a side of ire, and rain Pepto Bismo–laced punches down on these match-made-in-hell misses.

CRYSTAL GAYLE HAIR

PUNCH RATING

I love long hair, I really do, but a gal shouldn't have to worry about her drain-clogging coif clearing the toilet seat when she drops trou. When locks are skimming the floor, it's not a hairstyle as much as a chairstyle. Tie the ends to a tree and relax in your portable hammock.

FACT OF THE MATTER

The longest hair on record goes to Xie Qiuping of China, whose rope of hair measures more than eighteen feet long. That's just greedy, as this Asian Rapunzel could provide for more than twenty wigs through Locks of Love.

Calf- or knee-length hair ain't pretty—there's a good two feet of split ends going on down there—and neither are your deep-seeded neuroses. You're wearing your insecurity, not on your sleeve, but on your head. Put your follicular folly in a ponytail, snip it off, and ship it off to Locks of Love. If you don't, my fist will make your brown eyes black and blue.

CYBER PDA

PUNCH RATING

I think it's sweet that you love each other, I really do. I'm happy to see status updates, tweets, and blog posts about your courtship, engagement, and wedding. Not only can I handle it, I'm heartened by it.

But my support of your relationship does not mean I want to be slimed with your cyber makeout sessions, your oversharing, and those sweet nothings all goddamned day. Tweeting about how much you miss your flaxen-haired beauty—even though you've only been apart an hour (which I know because you tweeted that, too)—or updating your Facebook status to detail what an incredible night you had with your Sweetpea or Huggy Bear makes me, in this order, 1) roll my eyes, 2) choke back my breakfast, and 3) want to share the love. Specifically, I dream of playing Cupid, pulling out a crossbow, and piercing you through the heart, or at least your fingers.

> **FACT OF THE MATTER**
> **As a term of endearment, "honey" dates back to ancient Greece. Sweet. You know what's not so sweet? Dropping "honey bunny" bombs toward your significant other all over Facebook.**

Take a note from Shakespeare: Speak low if you speak love. In other words, keep it in your pants and send your true love an e-mail. We don't want to see that sap. That's what porn, Jane Austen novels, and Reese Witherspoon movies are for.

DECEPTIVELY BAD PRODUCE

PUNCH RATING

Scene: Kitchen. Mouthwatering smells are emanating from all corners of the room. In the center, an impeccably dressed, radiant hostess prepares to cut into an avocado. Guests are due to arrive in minutes.

> **FACT OF THE MATTER**
> **To suss out if an avocado is rotten, pull off the stem. If the end is mushy, black, or mildewed, you're hosed.**

Ten seconds later: "Are you #$%^&*$#Q@% kidding me?" The hostess surveys the decay that has reared its fugly head on her cutting board.

The avocado is rotten.

As you can imagine, this romantic comedy just became a tragedy.

When the farmers' market is closed during winter, I shop at the grocery store. I take my time in the produce department, thumping, sniffing, and pinching, trying to suss out freshness. Apparently, I suck at this.

I pick out avocados that seem destined for my delicious guacamole, only to cut into them and find them rotten. I peel an orange and find it devoid of any juice. Tomatoes, watermelon, and all manner of fruits find their way into my kitchen and then into the compost pail. Don't even mention a mealy apple in my presence.

Aside from the disappointment, these douchebag foodstuffs cut into my budget. I invested in that jicama and it totally hosed me.

A good piece of fruit can transform my day from mediocre to magical, and conversely, one bad apple can spoil my lunch...and the whole damn day. I want payback. I want to beat black-hearted produce into a bloody pulp.

DREAM CATCHERS

PUNCH RATING

Outside of the reservation and 1979, a dream catcher is just plain dumb. Hung on a rearview mirror or as living room art, it deserves to be punched in its sinewy face. What made you think this was a good idea? Did you powwow with a shaman in a sweat lodge? Were you trippin' on peyote with Val Kilmer?

While I was curiously drawn to the feathered roach clips on sale at the Berrien County Youth Fair back in the '80s, I backed away. I didn't smoke the wacky tobackey and my name wasn't Stands with a Pan-Indian Tchotchke in her Fist (although that would have been so fucking rad). Even then, I knew dream catchers sucked it hard.

FACT OF THE MATTER

Dream catchers grab nightmares in their web, while good dreams find their way through the holes to the sleeping person below via the feathery fringe. I don't know if it works when it's hanging from a rearview mirror, unless the driver is asleep at the wheel.

Dream catchers were traditionally hung over a bed to protect papooses from nightmares. Um, sorry to break it to you, you woo-woo kookaloo, but you just conjured up the bad dream that is me. While listening to some sweet nature sounds with a backing woodlands flute, I am going to tie a stick to your Southwestern Spirograph and thrash you within an inch of your life.

The American Indian wasn't crying over pollution in that 1970s ad; he saw the writing—and your ridiculous dream catcher—on the wall.

DUCK FACE

PUNCH RATING

I've done it. I don't know why.

Maybe I was going for a *Real Housewives* blowfish look and was trying to mask my lack of Juvederm or lip implants. Maybe I was blowing a kiss to the cameraman. Maybe I was just knee-deep in gin.

Maybe, but more likely, I was going for sexy and thought duck face was a quick way to look like I was single and ready to mingle. Instead, I—and every other trout mouth out there—looked like I had a bill instead of lips, like I was ready to sample some sardines instead of a tasty man's mouth.

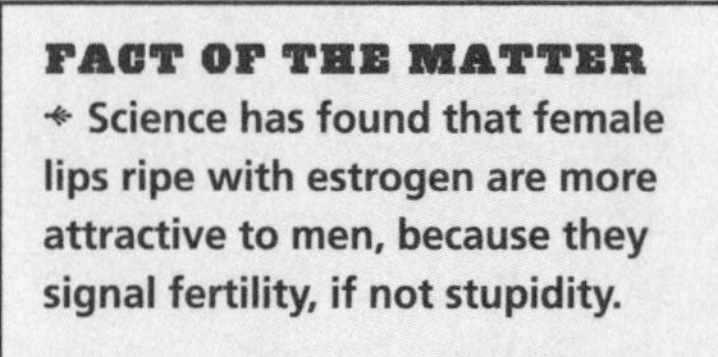

FACT OF THE MATTER

Science has found that female lips ripe with estrogen are more attractive to men, because they signal fertility, if not stupidity.

I don't want to ruffle any feathers, but ladies, when a camera is pulled out, please remember "quack is whack."

EARLY BIRDS

PUNCH RATING 👊👊

Whenever I have unhappily stumbled into an office or coffee shop at 7 a.m., I see a flock of smug early birds silently congratulating each other for being such productive, rarified members of society. These chipper toolboxes are one step away from developing a secret handshake. This sort of self-satisfaction would be irksome enough, but add to that their silent disdain for anyone who sets their alarm for sometime after sunrise and they really make me want to flip my shit.

Dude, so you get to your desk at the ass-crack of dawn. You are the first one to turn off the security alarm. You regularly meet with your trainer at 5:30 a.m. You have special alone time with the boss. Whoopadeedoo! The only thing this means is that you go to bed at 9 p.m. You climb under the covers before the sun goes down, which is not something to pat yourself on the back about, unless you're a farmer.

> **FACT OF THE MATTER**
> **The poster child of early birds, larks are diurnal, meaning that they at their liveliest from sunrise to sunset.**

Don't give me the stinkeye when I roll in. Don't even hint that I don't work hard for the money. I usually toil away until I turn off the lights long after midnight, so eat my alarm clock. We have different schedules, different rhythms that suit us. It doesn't mean that your day is any longer or more fruitful than mine. It just means that you're a judgmental fuck who drinks decaf after 2 p.m.

The best part of waking up is piping hot Folgers in your face.

EVER-PRESENT BLUETOOTH

PUNCH RATING

Are you a cyborg? Ari Gold? A sex phone operator? No?

Too bad.

If you were, I might give your face a pass (particularly if you're a T-800), but now I'm going to have to give you a smackdown that will leave you black and Bluetoothless. I know the frequency, Kenneth, and you and I are on different wavelengths.

The 2012 version of a pager clipped to your waist, an eew-tooth not only receives messages, it sends one. It communicates one thing loud and clear: YOU'RE A MASSIVE TOOL.

FACT OF THE MATTER

Bluetooth isn't just a catchy amalgam; it's actually the anglicized version of Blåtand/Blåtann. This was the epithet of Harald I, a tenth-century badass who united various Danish tribes into a single kingdom, probably punching a few faces in his process.

If you have to try that hard to look important, chances are you're not. Unless you're driving or performing surgery or tracking down Sarah Conner, stuff that thing in your pocket. Heck, clip it to your belt. Maybe I'll think it's a pager, which is almost old-school cool by comparison. Almost.

EXCESSIVE PUNCTUATION

PUNCH RATING

I get it!!! I really do!!! Srsly!!!!!!!!!!!!!!

I know you're excited or scared or confused or slumped over the keyboard so your ear keeps hitting the question mark key. There's no need to drive home the point by slapping me in the face with punctuation marks or poking me in the eye with those goddamn extraneous exclamation points.

I'm a big advocate of everything in moderation and yep, that applies to my semicolons. Ever since high school, I figured there was a perfect way to express anything through words. Words. Not punctuation. Spend more time conveying what you mean through language, please, and leave those poor, defenseless exclamation marks alone. What did they ever do to you?

> **FACT OF THE MATTER**
> **An exclamation point or exclamation mark is also called a bang and a dembanger, the latter of which I'm thinking should be my drag queen name.**

F. Scott Fitzgerald said, "Cut out all those exclamation marks. An exclamation mark is like laughing at your own jokes." Word, Fitz, word. Can you imagine the difference it would make if he had thrown in one or several exclamation points to his otherwise gorgeous WASPy text, such as when Gatsby describes Daisy?

The original: "Her voice is full of money."

The icky: "Her voice is full of money!!!"

A beautiful observation becomes the sort of squawking, self-congratulatory promise that a Shamwow ad delivers. Less is more. Period.

FLAVOR SAVERS

PUNCH RATING

Frankly, I'm stumped. What's the thought process behind the crumb catcher that's also known as a soul patch? I wish I was a passenger on that train of thought....

It'll make me look handsome, slimmer, younger, cooler, douchier...

Clearly, there has to be intent behind the soul thatch, since it's groomed and shaped to within a hair of its life. Are you trying to lengthen your face? Did you need an arrow to find your mouth? Did you slip with the razor and have to keep on pruning? Whatever the case, I have to break it to you: Dude, you're sporting a bikini wax on your chin.

Be it the Frito or Dorito, you've got a landing strip on your face. Runways belong at O'Hare, not on your nearly hairless mug. Only Bruce Springsteen can pull that shit off, and, while he was born to run, he's still skating on thin ice. Embrace the Brazilian. It'll only hurt for a minute. However, if you keep that thin dead line on your puss, you're in for a world of pain as I wax, thread, sugar, and shave your face, all the while withholding the Ibuprofen. Just call me a flavor shaver.

FACT OF THE MATTER

Jazz musicians of the 1950s and '60s sported soul patches, giving me yet another reason to punch jazz in the face, specifically the chin.

FOODIES

PUNCH RATING

Don't sniff it, don't eyeball it, don't comment on how it's plated like a pagoda or a Zen garden, don't detail the 39 steps it took to make it, don't start comparing it to the meal you had at El Bulli, and don't complain about the new chef while alternately giving me his culinary CV.

I don't want to hear it. I just want to eat it.

I love food as much as the next person. I like food the way Homer likes his doughnuts.

But a food snob I am not. You'll never find me asking whether my Copper River salmon was gill-netted and bled and dressed on site. I'll never lift a fiddlehead fern and wax rhapsodic about hunting the zenmai in East Asia during a trip with Anthony Bourdain. I'll fork that fern and put it where it belongs: my belly.

Don't put nettle pasta on a pedestal, put it in your piehole. After all, it's food. You're supposed to eat it, not dissect it.

Sometimes, I just want to eat a box of mac 'n cheese, and not the Annie's kind. And I don't need you to tell me how to zest it up with Emmentaler and linguiça. Don't take the comfort out of my food or I might have to bust out the mandoline and create a new dish of hurt.

FACT OF THE MATTER

According to The World's 50 Best Restaurants website, the number-one restaurant in the world in 2012 was Denmark's Noma. Mmm, Nordic cuisine.

THE GENIUS BAR

PUNCH RATING

ME: "Why do I want to punch the Genius Bar in the face?"

SIRI: "I have a fishbowl punch located on the menu at the Genie Bar. Do you want directions?"

> **FACT OF THE MATTER**
> **Genius Bars have been stroking egos and touch pads since 2001; they are headed up by a Lead Genius, who should take off his glasses and wait for my iPunch.**

I'm a longtime Apple-only user. I know a few key commands, I can solve most glitches on my own, and some friends even ask me for Mac advice. I used to believe all this was sort of a "na-nu na-nu" secret handshake into the cool kids' club. Heck, I even wear interesting eyewear, for the love of Steve Jobs. Prescription eyewear, bitches.

But when I mosey up to the Apple Store's Genius Bar, my illusion/delusion is shattered. I'm not nerdy cool. I'm a tool. My only consolation is that I'm beta-lame, while everyone ahead of me in line is a 2.0 tool (in fact, they might be cyborgs). I have a lot of time to observe these bearded, iPadded creatures in their natural habitapp, seeing as my Casio just went from 3:00 to 3:45—Cupertino time—while I wait for assistance on a stool clearly imported from the distant future.

It doesn't take a genius to figure out that Apple is shamelessly trying to stroke my ego, whispering in my ear like a 21st-century iAgo. There's no need to make me feel like a Mensa member just because I belly up to the bar; my IQ score did that for me in fifth grade. Bitches.

GPS ADDICTS

PUNCH RATING

"What are you doing?"
"I'm putting the restaurant we're going to into my GPS."
"Um...it's a half-mile down this road."

Shuttle and cab drivers, go right ahead and go crazy with the positioning systems. Maybe the route from the airport won't be quite as circuitous (and pricey) with some help from above. On a long road trip, go ahead and bust it out. I'm all for things that make life easier. But some geographically challenged chumps seem to be using GPS to find their own ass.

You've lived in this neighborhood for years, Lostco de Gama. You don't appear to have suffered a crushing blow to the head resulting in temporary global amnesia. So why on earth do you turn to a bossy machine to get anywhere and everywhere? Why do you require assistance to drive in a straight line, Christopher Coldumbass? High school geometry must have been a real bitch. Word problems probably sent you into the fetal positioning system.

> **FACT OF THE MATTER**
> ✦ **The most popular GPS voice belongs to a slightly bossy and therefore hot Australian woman.**
>
> **FACT OF THE MATTER**
> ✦ **GPS is maintained by the U.S. government; it became fully operational in 1994.**

Why do you need a disembodied automaton with an Australian accent to tell you what to do? That's what a dominatrix is for, duh. And I'm right here in the passenger seat, ready and willing to tell you where to get off, if you get my drift.

GROCERY BAG GUILT

PUNCH RATING

I'm a bad citizen of the earth. I admit it. When I walk out the door, I don't always know that I'm going to wind up at the grocery store, and consequently, I might not have any sort of bag, basket, bowl, or tray with which to carry my groceries home. So sue me (or charge me that annoying five cents per bag that you're itching to).

I feel like a total hosebag when I skulk—bagless—toward the cashier to ring up my snacklets. I start apologizing to the employee, who really couldn't care less if I take home eleven plastic bags.

FACT OF THE MATTER

✧ **In 2009, the U.S. International Trade Commission reported that the nation uses 102 billion bags each year.**

My carbon footprint is pretty damn small even if my hooves are a healthy 9 1/2. I use public transportation, my pad is tiny, I turn out the lights, I recycle.

I use plastic bags as trashcan liners and paper bags for recycling, and yet my guilt persists, which seriously pisses me off. And there are a lot of green assholes—grassholes—ready to pass judgment on me and my bag stash. I've seen the stinkeye in the checkout line, believe me.

I have taken steps toward assuaging my guilt. Over the past year or so, I've accumulated quite a few market bags. I bought one I thought was cute, I was given a couple, and I even made an adorable bag as a craft project for a book. But do I remember to take them with me?

Nay.

So I'm left with a wad of plastic bags and a serious resentment toward my inner grasshole. Something must be done: dropkicking my grocery-bag guilt to the curb…into a recycling bin, of course.

HAIR EXTENSIONS

PUNCH RATING 👊👊👊

I blame Paris Hilton. Thanks to her, a whole generation of skanks and trophy wives with French tips and tennis bracelets have embraced a culture of fake. They've embraced hair extensions.

Hair has become an accessory, like a pair of earrings or shoes, that you can just don and doff at will. Hair used to be a gal's crowning glory; now it's just a stringy hat.

It used to be that people would hide the artificial, be it boobs, a tan, or hair. Bragging rights came from things being real. While Crystal Gayle's hair could have been used to garrote her, do you think she'd be caught dead with extensions? Her long hair was noteworthy because it was real.

FACT OF THE MATTER

At the Tirumala Tirupati Devasthanams temple in India, some 10,000 to 12,500 Hindu pilgrims offer their hair daily. Their shorn locks are then sold for premium extensions, netting up to $15 million annually for the temple.

Back away from the Jessica Simpson clip-in hairdon't and work with what you've got. Short hair? Now that's hot. For reals.

HAYDEN CHRISTENSEN AS ANAKIN SKYWALKER

PUNCH RATING

I waited almost thirty years to see Anakin get his Vader on. Instead, I was subjected to Christensen's whiney little bitch with bad hair and a slightly congested voice. If being jealous and misguided were enough to turn someone to the Dark Side, we'd all be lousy with the Force.

Anakin wasn't supposed to be Emo, he was supposed to be fucking E-V-I-L. Slink off to Tatooine, keep a dream journal, front a band, and stop washing your hair. Torture the Republic with your music if you have to, but get over yourself, Little Orphan Ani. You're no more than Chancellor Palpatine's butt boy.

The only satisfying thing about *Revenge of the Sith* was seeing you lying there without arms or legs as the magma inched closer. Since the lava flow and Obi-Wan didn't quite finish you off, you pissy wet noodle with light saber envy, let me inflict some additional pain in exchange for the 140 minutes of cinematic torture I endured. Let the Death Star that is my fist rain fury on your respirator, and may the Force be with me.

FACT OF THE MATTER

- Christensen won a Golden Raspberry award for Worst Supporting Actor for *Episode II: Attack of the Clones,* beating out such stiff competition as Freddie Prinze Jr. in *Scooby-Doo.*

HORROR MOVIE TRAILERS

PUNCH RATING 👊👊

I'm home, minding my own business. The front door is locked, the windows secure. I'm wearing my jammies.

And then, unexpectedly, I'm violated. By my television.

I might be innocently watching the nightmare that is *Jersey Shore* or a grisly autopsy on *CSI* when the show cuts to a commercial. Sigh. Instead of a Cover Girl ad, it's a goddamned horror movie trailer. A young girl is running in the woods, presumably away from a psychopath or the not-so-Steadicam that's hunting her down. In just two minutes, I hear screaming and I see duct tape, knives, guns, sweaty unshaved faces, moody lighting, fear, choppy editing, a microwave....

My heart is racing and I'm seriously disturbed.

It's coming from inside the house. Like Drew Barrymore in the opening sequence of *Scream*, I can't escape. It's bad enough that *Friday the 13th* forever screwed my chances for a fear-free camping trip, but now I have to be afraid every time I reach for the remote. The obvious solution is to quickly turn the channel or turn off the TV before I punch it in its liquid crystal display. Fuck that. These trailers make me mad as hell and I'm not going to take it any more.

It's time to turn the tables on my tormentors. I'm going to enlist that demon chicklet in need of a deep conditioner and a comb from *The Ring* to help. Samara could crawl into the TV and magnetize anything that triggers my gag reflex.

FACT OF THE MATTER

Part of the reason TV commercials seem louder than the program you were just watching is that you were probably listening to human voices, which don't have as much range as music and slasher audio effects. The horror, the horror.

IKEA HABITRAIL

PUNCH RATING

Confession: My apartment is lousy with IKEA. But it's not for any love for the brick-and-mortar store (or *butik*, to the Swedes out there).

Nr.

As I seek out my Malm bureau, I realize I should have picked up a bag of meatballs from the giant cooler in the Swedish Food Market so I could leave a trail. Even with the help of the signage that sprouts around every corner like skinny Kvart lampposts, I'm lost in the mousetrap, or should I say mousetråpp?

The IKEA habitrail is rivaled only by Gaylord Opryland Hotel, which still comes in as a distant second. They should just put a giant hamster wheel and a water dropper by the entrance and make it official. Clogged with kids hopped up on lingonberries and couples quarreling over the merits of Vanvik vs. Floro bed frames, the aisles of IKEA are sure to bring on a headache faster than the time it takes to fill up your cart with crap that's not on your list. Instead of monster bags of tealights, IKEA should fill the endcaps with bins of ibuprofen. Ädvil is a name that would be right at home in this Swedish funhouse; just don't forget the umlaut.

FACT OF THE MATTER

IKEA is an acronym using the initials of the founder's name, as well as the farm he grew up on and his hometown. Instead of determining your porn name, what's your IKEA name? (Initials, farm, hometown.) Mine would be JAWLS, or maybe JÄWLS.

INTENTIONALLY MISSPELLED TITLES

PUNCH RATING 👊👊👊👊

When asked by a national magazine why she named her album The Dutchess and not the proper "duchess," Fergie had this to say (hint: She's not from the Netherlands): "The spelling is different because I didn't want people who didn't know how to say it to call it 'the Douche-ess.'"

It gets better.

"I thought, 'Let me dumb-ify it a little bit.' Sometimes you smarten things up and get more clever with words. It's fun to go the other way, and it's always nice for people not to expect as much from me."

> **FACT OF THE MATTER**
> ✦ Quentin Tarantino had a few explanations about the spelling of *Inglourious Basterds*, saying once that it's a "Basquiat-esque touch." Um, no. It's a yambag touch. Jean-Michel was known for graffiti, not illiteracy.

Um, sweetcheeks, sorry to break it to you, but after "My Humps," I wasn't exactly expecting you to play chess with Bill Gates. But I did hope that you'd proofread the title of your CD.

Is it street to be stupid? Is it in vogue to be a low-forehead asshat? Call me nutbar, but why not use your celebrity to educate and elevate your audience? Why ya gotta be an inglourious basterd?

This sort of widespread dumbing-down interferes with my pursuit of happyness. And it certainly chaps my lovely lady lumps. I guess the only way to deal with these spellwreckers is to call in some Merriam and Webster to knock some sense—or at least an ability to spell the title of their album or film correctly—into them.

IT'S VERSUS ITS

PUNCH RATING

I could go on about my disdain for the wrong use of "there," "they're," and "their," or "hear" and "here," but what really drives me batshit crazy is the improper use of "its" and "it's." There is no reason that it's confusing. Seriously. If you fuck this up regularly, there is something wrong with you, you had a shitty teacher in junior high, or you just don't care, which is almost worse. Language is sacred to me. When you mangle "it," you figuratively shit all over my Strunk & White with your grammatical apathy.

> **FACT OF THE MATTER**
>
> **In the UK in 2009, the Birmingham City Council banned apostrophes from all public addresses, using the logic that no one understands how to use them properly. Way to pander to your less-gifted citizens.**

This is all you need to remember: If you can say "it is" instead of "it's" and it sounds right, then you should use an apostrophe. "It's" is a contraction and should ONLY ever be used that way.

For example:

It is raining men = It's raining men = Perfectamundo.
The rain in Spain falls mainly on it's plain = Just plain wrong.

If you need any further help remembering this, I can go Pavlov on your remedial English ass and inflict a little conditional response with my fist every time you bungle "its" usage. That should remedy the situation, don't you think?

JAZZ

PUNCH RATING

In general, I like to know where I'm going, be it a drive, a project, or a piece of music. Jazz fills me with agita. I don't know when it's going to end, and I don't know what the squirrelly fucker is going to pull next.

I have to say, I'm kind of blue about this. Unlike handlebar mustaches and mimes, I want to like jazz. I want to don a beret and sit in a dark club, nodding my head and saying things like, "yeah, man" and "dig that smooth groove." I used to think I wasn't smart enough to get jazz. Now I feel as if all the cool kids know the secret Herbie Hand(cock)shake and left me out of the Felonious Monk Memorial Clubhouse.

FACT OF THE MATTER

Duke Ellington said, "By and large, jazz has always been like the kind of a man you wouldn't want your daughter to associate with." Um, it's actually the music I don't want to associate with.

This only fuels my anger, which is swelling to the point where I want to give the Dave Brubeck Quartet a serious time out and inflict some damage on David Sanborn's reed. Scat needs to scram. You dig, Dizzy?

JUMPSUITS

PUNCH RATING 👊👊👊

It's tricky enough to go to the bathroom in a one-piece bathing suit. Why would you want to wear what's basically a body stocking out and about?

Think about it. If you have to take your top off to pee, you could easily drop a sleeve in the toilet…or get a chest cold. This fashion victim's onesie needs to hustle back to where it came from—1977, to be specific. Whether it's a strapless romper or an homage to skydiving style, chumpsuits belong on the trash heap of bad ideas (along with Utilikilts and mullets)…unless you are changing my oil.

> **FACT OF THE MATTER**
> **Unless you're rocking a colostomy bag, it's hard to see how wearing jumpsuits are a viable option for anyone with a challenging bladder.**

KIDDIE PAGEANTS

PUNCH RATING

> **FACT OF THE MATTER**
> **We spend our whole life trying to keep our teeth and avoid dentures. But pageant kids snap on a creepy set of false teeth jauntily called "flippers" to mask imperfect smiles.**

I don't know which is worse: the pageants, the parents, or the glassy-eyed kids. Wait, yes I do: It's the parents.

How any parent can dye their little girl's naturally preternatural locks boggles the mind. Women are forever trying to get an 8-year-old's natural highlights, and these momthras are frying everything good and holy from these tiny heads. Momsters brush mascara onto baby lashes and glop up little rosebud lips with lip gloss. These kids can't read *Vogue* yet, but they're more high maintenance than Anna Wintour. I bet they could even teach me how to apply liquid eyeliner properly.

The pageants themselves are beyond low budget. They're held on a rickety stage with a sad backdrop made with a glue gun, glitter, and an asswagon of prayer. The stage mommy sits in the audience, miming her kid's "talent" routine while her little girl preens, dances, smiles, and jazz hands her way through a treacly patriotic number.

The ragtag judges eat this shit up. I want to beat this shit up. I want to deprogram the little spray-tanned ventriloquist dummies by herding them into a lil' miss protection program. Here, in a home with no television or tiaras, they will play with crayons, not lip pencils, and draw outside the lines. The only Barbies in the house will be the ones manufactured by Mattel, not a mom from hell. And the mommies dearest will be beaten with a sack of those very same Barbie dolls while being forced to sing Aqua's "Barbie Girl" in a leotard. Being plastic isn't always fantastic.

KIDS' SONGS

PUNCH RATING

"Baaaaackpack, backpack!"
"Hot dog! I've got the rhythm in my head."
"There were ten in the bed and the little one said, 'Roll over, roll over.'"

Clearly, there are many problems with the above scenario (TEN in the bed? Are we in a Dickens novel?); however, the biggest beef I have is that I can't get the mother-lovin' song out of my head.

As much as I tried to sing "Doncha wish your baby was hot like me?" to my goddaughter, it's the wheels on the bus that go round and round in my head. A friend once instructed me to hum the *Entertainment Tonight* theme whenever I got stuck in an endless loop of song suckage. Happily, this worked for wrong songs from Sisqó, the Baha Men, and a musician ex-boyfriend, but kids' songs are more insidious. They appear innocent on the surface, which makes them all the more sinister (think of what happened to baby-face Anakin Skywalker if you need a cautionary tale).

This will not do.

Since shouting some 2 Live Crew or other material offensive to Tipper Gore's ears might stunt a toddler's growth, I propose that for every Wiggles or Little Einstein song we have to jazz hands our way through, they get to suffer the decidedly non-hummable sounds of early *American Idol* auditions. That's some aural poop that will never get stuck in anyone's cerebral sandbox.

FACT OF THE MATTER

While it seems to have been lodged in our hippocampus since birth, the earliest printing of "Row, Row, Row Your Boat" with lyrics and music as we know it goes back much further, dating to 1881.

KNIGHTED CELEBRITIES

PUNCH RATING

Hey you, with the fancy title and doodad pinned to your chest: Did you rescue a damsel in distress? Pull a sword out of a stone? Do battle in the name of the crown?

FACT OF THE MATTER
✦ **The Knight (or Dame) Grand Cross is the highest honor, resulting in an immediate "Sir" or "Dame" title before your name.**

No? What's that, you say? You played a vixen on *Dynasty* and bear responsibility for introducing shoulder pads to the 1980s? Showed your power by "Stayin' Alive" on the airwaves in 1977? Make expensive handbags that only royalty and Oprah can afford?

When Joan Collins, the Brothers Gibb (who really are Knights in White Satin), and Anya Hindmarch are getting knighted, call me a dissenter. It seems like the Queen is handing out Grand Cross stars right and left. Does she pick up the medals in bulk at Costco?

Sir Bono sounds like a fancy cut of bone-in meat at a steakhouse. Damn—ahem, Dame—Kylie Minogue apparently nabbed the Order of the British Empire for her "services to music." David Beckham, OBE? More like OMG. I think Henry Winkler is the bomb, but I don't see how the "thumbs up" merits a knighthood for the Fonz.

Your Majesty: I know it's fun to have some hip playmates who will show up at state functions wearing inappropriate clothing and serenade you with a rousing rendition of "Can't Get You Outta My Head," but you don't have to buy your way into the cool-kid crowd. Unless one of these celebrities figures out how to slay a dragon—and I'm not talking about kicking a mean drug habit or getting a full sleeve tattoo of Grendel—put down the medals and pick up the phone. I'm sure they'd come for the night.

LAST SWIG OF BEER

PUNCH RATING 👊👊👊

An ice-cold beer is the perfect complement to so many things: fish and chips, Polish sausage, my left hand. Couple my thirst for a cold one with slow service and my miserly nature, and you'll find me drinking every last drop from the bottle.

Herein lies the problem.

The last swig of beer is always, without fail, a disappointment, a letdown akin to hooking up with an ex or tracking down your high school crush. It's warm—you could heat a room with it. It's flat, like a soda that's been sitting on the counter for three days. And it's sour… like backwash. That last ill-advised sip leaves your mouth tasting faintly of hurl. In other words, it's puke-flavored broth. I don't know about you, but this isn't the taste I want left in my mouth at the end of the night, if you get my drift.

This afterwaste is going to get an afterlife. Being thrifty and shit, I'm pouring the dregs of every last bottle and can of PBR/MGD/IPA/BFD into a vat and repurposing this pukewarm swill to make bread or shampoo. Flat beer may bring me down, but damn if it doesn't fluff up my hair.

FACT OF THE MATTER

PBR is so named because it was inexplicably deemed "America's Best" at the 1893 Chicago World's Fair.

LIMP HANDSHAKES & WIMPY HUGS

PUNCH RATING

I dig a strong handshake. Mine is a point of pride, and I always extend my hand with intention and strength. I don't get folks who place their hand in mine and just leave it lying there, so I can hold their flaccid mitt. If I wanted a dead fish in my hand, I'd be down at the waterfront flirting with the fishmongers. If you're going to shake my hand, press the flesh like you mean business. I don't care if you have sweaty palms, raggedy cuticles, or aphephobia. I do care if you washed after peeing. If you can't muster up the energy to grip my hand and give it a few pumps, rest assured I'm going to curl that hand up and steer it in the direction of your face. So much for your fear of being touched. Touch my fist, friend.

> **FACT OF THE MATTER**
> **No surprise, but a University of Alabama study found folks with limp-wristed handshakes to be more neurotic and shy than their firm-handed counterparts. I would also add lame to the list.**

And if you're going to hug me, press your body against me properly so I can hook my leg around your ass. That's just good form. Don't lean in and pat me on the back without actually making contact with me. It either indicates that 1) I smell (which is clearly ridiculous), 2) you are afraid of my boobs (which is possible), or 3) you hate the idea of human contact. Embrace intimacy, embrace me. I won't bite (unless I really like you).

MAGIC 8 BALL

PUNCH RATING

Screw you, Magic 8 Ball, and your "Better not tell you now" coyness. You think you're so superior, telling us all what's what with your terse responses. Would it hurt you to give me an affirmative one of these days? I mean, I do my part. I focus, I shake, I beg, I plead, I stroke your smooth exterior. "Reply hazy try again," "Cannot predict now," and "Don't count on it" may be truthful, but would it hurt you to throw me a bone once in a while? Everyone knows that polite white lies are just good form if the truth is going to hurt. You don't see me telling you "My sources say you suck," do you? No, I keep it to myself, because I'm classy that way.

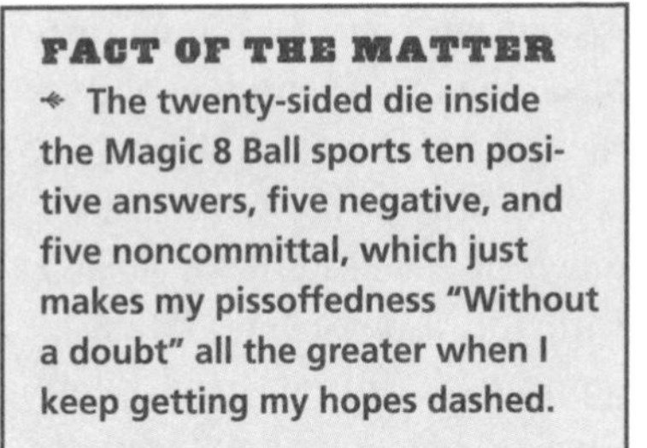

FACT OF THE MATTER

The twenty-sided die inside the Magic 8 Ball sports ten positive answers, five negative, and five noncommittal, which just makes my pissoffedness "Without a doubt" all the greater when I keep getting my hopes dashed.

You might as well just say "He's just not that into you" or "Poverty is in your future," stab me in the heart with a sharp point of your fickle icosahedral die, and be done with it. Stop prolonging the agony, or better yet, give me an "It is certain" or a simple "YES" every now and then, you smug ball of jackassedness.

MALAPROPISMS & MISPRONUNCIATIONS

PUNCH RATING

I've been a stickler for language since I was in seventh grade, which means I've been one persnickety fuck for decades. I try to tamp down my know-it-all-ness when a friend mangles the mother tongue (luckily I surround myself with smart people) but nevertheless, I internally cringe when someone busts out a malaprop or mispronounces a word.

There are words and phrases that have been around since the dawn of the Oxford English Dictionary, or at least since we've been alive. It's harder to forgive the repeated slip of the tongue. That makes me think you just don't give a rat's ass.

Or it makes me think that you're George W. Bush. Dear Mr. Presidon't, I'm so glad I no longer have to hear dimwitticisms like "We need an energy bill that encourages consumption" or "We cannot let terrorists and rogue nations hold this nation hostile." Dude, you went to Yale, for fuck's sake. Could you at least *try* to appear intelligent?

FACT OF THE MATTER

"Malapropism" traces its roots to Mrs. Malaprop, a character in a 1775 play, *The Rivals*, by Richard Brinsley Sheridan.

To me, the most oft-misused and ear-bleeding offense is "irregardless." When I worked at a publishing company, we editors would roll our internal eyes every time the owner threw that out in a meeting. Let me reiterate: I worked at a PUBLISHING company. Dude should have known better. Better yet, dude should have been punched in the face.

And if I hear someone bust out "nuculur," I'm going to mushroom cloud all over them, even if they were once president.

MAN CAVES

PUNCH RATING 👊👊👊

You man, me woman. I get it. It's not that hard to figure out our differences. You shave, I wax. You like *Red Dawn*, I dig *Dirty Dancing*. But when it comes to portioning off areas of the house, I don't see why you XYs need your own space to watch sports or porn or whatever it is you do in there. You don't need a separate hole to crawl into when you are discovering fire or sharpening tools. That's what the garage is for, Encino Man.

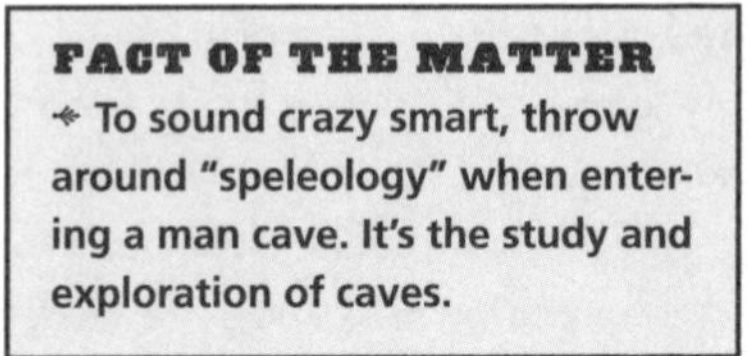
FACT OF THE MATTER
To sound crazy smart, throw around "speleology" when entering a man cave. It's the study and exploration of caves.

And your male room shouldn't be where the wagon-wheel coffee table goes to die; that's what Craigslist is for, buddy. Lose the threadbare recliner and put your collection of baseball caps or hockey jerseys in storage. Call me crazy, but clothing is meant to be put on the body, not hung on a wall.

I hate to break it to you, but you're not a caveman. You're a guy who hasn't shaved in three days. Wash off your Pleistocene funk, turn on the light, and for God's sake, stop grunting. If not, I'll have no choice but to whack you with a woolly mammoth bone, which is going to leave a mark, no matter how you try to cover it up with your loincloth.

MERCURY IN RETROGRADE

PUNCH RATING

I've been dreading this day for awhile. By most accounts, goddamned Mercury is going into retrograde again. What this means is that Mercury appears to us earthlings to slow down and move backwards for several weeks.

It also means that I'm fucked.

I am often suspicious of anything with a whiff of woo-woo, but over the years, I've learned to heed the power of this punk-ass planet. E-mails go missing, interpersonal communication goes down the crapper, misunderstandings abound, business deals fall through, my motherfucking motherboard dies. It's around this time that I turn to the bottle.

How this little bitch planet wields so much impish power is beyond me, as well as people a whole lot higher than me on the intellectual food chain. The one thing I do know is that this ass-illogical shit has got to stop. I think a call to NASA is in order. Maybe if we can hit it hard enough with a monster missile, we can change its orbit and stop the insanity.

FACT OF THE MATTER

In Roman mythology, Mercury is the messenger of the gods, and for some reason the planet seems to wreak havoc on communication and relationships when it's in retrograde.

But until we make that happen, back your files up...seriously.

MIMES

PUNCH RATING

Well, if you insist.

These blanc buffoons place themselves in my line of ire the minute they rock the whiteface. Dammit to hell, Marcel Marceau! What have you wrought?

Riddle me curious, but what compels a kookaloo (in French, *kookalou*) to tumble down the rabbit hole and sign up for a mime class? Did he have a grandparent who always seemed to have trouble with his invisible umbrella on windy days? Did she see a Doug Henning television special in the '70s that made her hot for French sailor shirts? Does he think miming will lend him a certain *je ne sais quoi*? I do know what: *Il est stupide.*

Mimes need to be rounded up and herded into a box in front of the Centre Pompidou. Tag these douchebaguettes with a black-and-white computer chip. And if anyone tries to escape the box, imaginary or otherwise, I'm going to throw back a *pain au chocolat* before going *un peu* Marquis de Sade on the rogue clown by choking him with his fey neckerchief. There won't be a need to draw a sad clown teardrop near his right eye. Those tears will be real, *mon ami.*

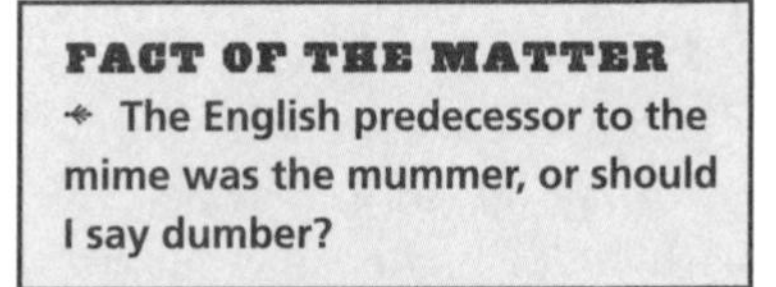
FACT OF THE MATTER

✦ The English predecessor to the mime was the mummer, or should I say dumber?

Clowns may be creepy, but mimes are the fiends who moonwalk through my nightmares.

MIRRORLESS DRESSING ROOMS

PUNCH RATING 👊👊👊👊

Mirror, mirror, on the wall, should I buy this dress? What's your call?

Cricket. Cricket.

There's no mirror in sight, not even of the fat or funhouse variety. Are you trying to be merciful, preventing me from seeing a fashion misstep? Nay, I think you have something more insidious in mind.

Here I am, stuck in this crawlspace of a dressing room, shimmying into some garment. If I miraculously manage to zip, hook, and button everything, I'd actually like to see how I look in it. But if I slink out to the communal mirror to eyeball the damage, sycophantic sales associates slither up, doing their best to convince me that sausage casing is the new black.

Yeah, no.

To be fair, there might be other reasons you tricked out your store with closets instead of dressing rooms. You might have broken your last mirror and are only two years into your seven years of bad luck. Maybe you're Medusa and want to make sure no one has a reflective surface when you're trying to turn them to stone. Or you might just be cheap.

But I think the most likely reason that the mirror has no place is that you're trying to be wily, flushing me out of the retail brush so you can get me in your sights and kill me with false compliments.

It's time to fight back. I think I should call upon the evil queen from *Snow White*, who knows a thing or two about the power of reflection. She can turn you into a wizened old witch in a bad dress and hair desperately in need of conditioner. Reflect on that.

MOLLY RINGWALD'S PROM DRESS IN PRETTY IN PINK

PUNCH RATING

Biggest. Cinematic. Letdown. Ever.

After showing mad personal style throughout the entire movie (no one, and I mean no one, rocks pearls and flowered fabric like Molly Ringwald), the girl shows up defiantly at prom to prove to the world and to Blaine, the insipid boy with the crazy eyes and white pleated pants, that she's not broken.

Um, it's just a thought, but she might have chosen a more suitable dress to take a stand in, something that didn't scream "home-sewn hot mess."

Andie should have left Fiona's dress alone. I want to bitch slap that polyester Frankenfrock with the collar and mesh insert, shred it, and burn it. Oh, wait—it's probably treated with flame retardant. Fire bad.

Let's hope Andie got that scholarship and used it at FIT or Parsons.

FACT OF THE MATTER

Costume designer Marilyn Vance worked on some of my all-time favorite movies, including *Die Hard, Road House, The Untouchables, Pretty Woman,* and *The Breakfast Club*, which makes her apromination almost forgivable. Almost.

MOTEL ART

PUNCH RATING

When visiting Fallingwater a few years back, a guide told us that Frank Lloyd Wright designed low ceilings and lots of windows into the famous home so people would be encouraged to go outside.

> **FACT OF THE MATTER**
> ✦ **The working-class classic *Dogs Playing Poker* actually refers to nine oils in a series of sixteen paintings by C.M. Coolidge. They were commissioned in 1903 to advertise cigars. You'd think one image of a bulldog puffing on a stogie would be more than enough.**

Well, motel art is about as far away as you can get from FLW, but the result is the same. I want to flee the premises when I am in a motel room dripping with bad art.

But first, I go into the bathroom to see if my eyes are bleeding.

Thomas Kinkade–like landscapes, art that is reminiscent of the cover of Duran Duran's "Rio," prints of ships and sandpipers, still lifes that match the bedspread—it's all one stinky art fart. Motel rooms are where art goes to die a slow, faded, badly framed death.

Next time, don't take an Ambien to get to sleep. Take down the art, turn it around, and stick it in the closet next to the ironing board. You'll sleep like a baby.

MR. DARCY

PUNCH RATING

Over the years, I've been sucked in again and again by your sang-froid, your stateliness, your brooding tall, dark, and handsomeness, and your ability to make me hot just by climbing out of your pond, soaking wet and fully clothed.

Since you are, well, not real, I've looked from here to Hampshire for a flesh-and-blood Fitzwilliam. I have not fared well. I entertained one yahoo because I thought he'd look dashing astride a horse wearing one of those long coats you fancy. I swoon at the thought of those things, the way they sweep the ground as you walk with determination, legs encased in breeches and knee boots....

I digress.

I dated another gentleman who, like you, was sensitive and felt deeply. But he didn't act on shit. He just stewed in his emo juices. Miserly compliments and infrequent attentions kept me wondering about his intentions until he laissez-faired us to death. I mean, how long is a girl supposed to hang in there, in hopes of securing moody blues like you?

Let's not forget the know-it-all narcissist who had clearly spent some time at Pemberley in your company. He was a real treat, spamming familiars and strangers with his prideful advice and prejudiced judgment. Proclamations as pillow talk don't exactly blow my petticoat up, sir.

Darcy, you're a prick. You don't like to dance. You throw your best friend around like a ventriloquist's dummy, telling him what to do and say. Bingley's one step away from sitting on your lap. Not cool. You publicly skewer a gal for her lack of connections and lowly parentage—we can't get enough of that—while secretly admiring her moxie and form. You bottle up your feelings until they bubble over and you blurt out your affections, telling her you love her despite your better judgment. Be still, my heart. This is going to catch a lady off guard, particularly since she's spent nigh on a year avoiding you, wondering what she ever did to irk your shit, and thinking you're a grade-A, navel-gazing jackwipe.

Yeah, you came through in the end, saving the Bennet family from social disgrace and all that. Always the hero, Mr. Darcy, you've ruined me for the real world of dating. No man can measure up and yet, I don't want to hold them to your standard, since you—how can I put this delicately?—suck.

You've screwed me, and, indeed sir, not in a good way.

FACT OF THE MATTER

Get this: A sex pheromone in male mouse urine (you didn't expect that, did you?) was named Darcin in honor of Mr. Darcy. Sort of takes the piss out of my punch, doesn't it?

NAKED PREGNANCY PORTRAITS

PUNCH RATING 👊👊👊👊

You're gorgeous and juicy, ladyfriend, but you're not Demi Moore. I don't want to see you naked when you're not pregnant. I sure as shit don't want to see you drop trou with a bun in the oven.

> **FACT OF THE MATTER**
> **Demi Moore starred in the mother of all pregnancy portraits, snapped by Annie Leibovitz in 1991 for the cover of *Vanity Fair.***

I don't have a problem with you hiring Annie Leibovitz to capture this oh-so-important period in your life. Just don't ask me to pore over the album, attend the portrait unveiling, or suffer your new two-for-one Facebook photo.

Treacly pregnancy photos bring navel gazing to a new level. Literally. In fact, your new outie is all you can see. Don't get me wrong: I can't wait to see the new addition to your family. In the meantime, just show me the sonogram.

NAMASTE

PUNCH RATING

When I hear someone say "namaste," I want to beat them and their sustainable clothing with a rain stick. I mean, fine, say it at the end of yoga class...if you absolutely have to. But when I hear it outside of the ashram, it harshes my mellow. The likely culprits are people who get their kids hopped up on carob chips and let them run around Trader Joe's because they are "spirited."

FACT OF THE MATTER

✦ **Like "aloha," namaste is both a greeting and farewell in India.**

FACT OF THE MATTER

✦ **The pressed-palms namaste bow appeared 4,000 years ago on clay seals, just proving that a lot of generations have escaped my wrath through the peace that comes with death.**

Namaste means "The light in me honors the light in you." When I'm in shavasana (during my rare forays into yoga) and I hear this, I throw up a little in my mouth. Laying on my back, well, you can imagine that this isn't a good thing. The light in me wants to knock your lights out or, better yet, reach in and rip out your heart chakra. Saying "namaste" doesn't make you enlightened, it just makes you a tool in an organic bamboo hoodie.

NAVEL LINT

PUNCH RATING 👊👊👊

Cue bombchickabowbow porn music. Turn the lights down. It's time to get busy. In other words, it's ON.

And as I go south, it's suddenly, screechingly OFF. Like nine kinds of OFF.

> **FACT OF THE MATTER**
> As an additional incentive to wash your nooks and crannies, know that 60 to 100 types of bacteria, yeasts, and fungi live inside the average belly button.

I was sorta hoping that your body would be a wonderland. Instead, it's a toxic waste dump up in there. Are you hoarding food or insulating for a hard winter? Check your nooks and crannies, people. Smelly belly button crud is a definite downer, and its presence will ensure that no one will want to travel down your yummy trail.

Rinsing does not a shower make.

NEW YEAR'S EVE

PUNCH RATING

New Year's Eve is always memorable. To wit:

1970-SOMETHING: Mom and Dad went to some party at the Holiday Inn and left me at home with my two older brothers. My Mrs. Beasley doll was decapitated that night, a harbinger of the tragic NYEs that were to come.

1989: I was freshly heartbroken and covering the Rose Bowl for the Michigan yearbook, so I was in L.A. with the staff photographer. We wound up at a giant alumni NYE party in the Valley, where I ran into my ex-boyfriend with his new girlfriend. I spent the night walking around the party with a twelve-pack, dispensing beers to people who had a reason to live. I then sped back to the hotel on one of the freeways in a fugue state, stayed up all night, and then downed gallons of black coffee in the Rose Bowl press box...where I was seated next to my ex, a sports editor for the university newspaper. Oh, and Michigan lost that year.

1990: This year found me in Detroit, partying it up with my college friends at a shindig at the top of the RenCen. I wish I could say I was drunk. I went up a down escalator...or tried to. After a scary ambulance ride to Detroit Receiving with a driver who resembled Large Marge, I spent five hours getting my Frankenknee stitched up while surrounded by an urban version of Hieronymus Bosch's "Garden of Earthly Delights." I couldn't bend my knee for two weeks.

2003: Fast forward a decade and change, and you'd find me at Bob & Barbara's, a dope dive bar in Philly, watching my boyfriend kiss a guy in front of me. I walked out and left him behind. I wish I had the sense to ditch New Year's Eve as well.

2004: Got stoned with my best friend while teaching her to knit and watching *Gigli*. This officially marked my march into spinsterdom.

FACT OF THE MATTER

✦ We have the Scots to thank for more than kilts; "Auld Lang Syne" is a Scots poem by Robert Burns set to a traditional folk song. Tartan-colored crap.

2008: Me, a sorta boyfriend (who drank too much and eventually passed out), and two gay bears sat on the couch and watched *Mythbusters*. Holla. Oh yeah, he broke things off the next week via IM. This really set the tone for the massive suck that was 2009.

In short, New Year's Eve should be forgotten and never brought to mind.

NEW YORKER CARTOONS

PUNCH RATING 👊👊👊👊

I have never, ever subscribed to *The New Yorker.*

There. I said it.

Call me unsophisticated, a troglodyte, a knob, whatev. I'm okay with it. I read *The Pew Yorker* occasionally when hanging out with friends more refined than me. But after eyeballing an issue, I walk away. It makes me feel stupid, and I'm already full up in that department.

It's not the articles. I can deal with a lengthy piece now and again, and I'm always able to soldier through "Shouts & Murmurs" and reviews with little damage to my ego.

And it's not the pompous Mr. Peanut dandy who represents. I get it. Dudes with monocles read *The New Yorker.* As they should. It's their thing, along with spats and a penchant for crème brûlée (not to mention words using the accent aigu).

It's the goddamn cartoons. When I'm in a dentist's office, I'd still rather reach for *Highlights* than *The New Yorker*. I can always detect what doesn't belong in a picture but fuck if I know what is clever or funny about a cartoon of a dude who, while raking leaves, holds up a maple leaf and says to his wife, "They're all pretty, but this one is my favorite." Am I missing something? Like IQ points or my frontal lobe? I'd like to change this caption to read: "You know, this could be dipped in resin or metal to make a five-pointed weapon to kill me with." That I would understand. That I could get behind.

FACT OF THE MATTER

↞ *The New Yorker* and its cartoons have been confounding folks since the magazine's inception in 1925. The most reprinted cartoon is Peter Steiner's 1993 drawing of two dogs in a front of a computer with the caption, "On the Internet, nobody knows you're a dog." That, I get.

NON-PRESCRIPTION EYEGLASSES

PUNCH RATING

Guess what? I'm selfish.

I'm also blind as a bat. I've worn -12.5 Coke bottles over my eyes since second grade. It makes me blind with rage when I see hipsters trying to look emo, ironic, brainy, sexy librarianish, or Weezery by donning a pair of frames.

If you don't need them as your third and fourth eyes, if your peepers don't look like tiny blinking specks or giant dilated saucers behind your lenses, back away from the Oliver Peoples and pass by Pearl Vision.

Buy a hat or get a tattoo, and let me have this.

FACT OF THE MATTER

I once had a date ask me to take off my glasses to see if my eyes were really that small. No, jackass. It's just that my prescription is -12.5...like your IQ.

OLD-GUY FACELIFTS

PUNCH RATING

It's hard to watch anything related to the Kardashians, not because they disgust me or because I think there's no collective there there. It's because of Bruce Jenner.

I remember the 1976 Olympics. I remember Jenner taking a victory lap after winning the decathalon, which was fitting during a Bicentennial Year. Proud to be an American, I ate a lot of Wheaties with Jenner on the box.

> **FACT OF THE MATTER**
> **If you suspect a full-on facelift, check for scars near the ears. Then take aim and create a new wrinkle in time.**

Now, I want to throw up my breakfast when I see Jenner doddering around the Kardashian klan. He looks like the grim reaper, the skin of his face pulled tightly over his cheekbones and implants. And he's not alone. Michael Douglas, Paul McCartney, and Steven Tyler are also part of the cryptkeeper club, not content to age gracefully, let alone move their face. These dudes are starting to look like ladies, and not in a good way. I'd punch them in the face, but I might shatter them.

OLD-GUY PONYTAILS

PUNCH RATING

Dude, don't you know that size—or in this case, length—doesn't matter?

When I see someone sporting a tired, scraggly ponytail, I have to muster every bit of self-control not to whip out some scissors and cut off that last stand of I don't know what. They're usually more frayed than a jute rope and have more split ends than Courtney Love eleven days into a psychotic break. I don't get the point. Mullets at least have that "business in the front, party in the back" thing going on. What can you say about a man with a mangy ponyfail? Hippie in the front, dying hippie in the back? Often, the ponytail accompanies a balding pate, which, guess what?, isn't fooling anyone. No amount of length on your last 134 strands will compensate for the loss of hair everywhere else on your dome.

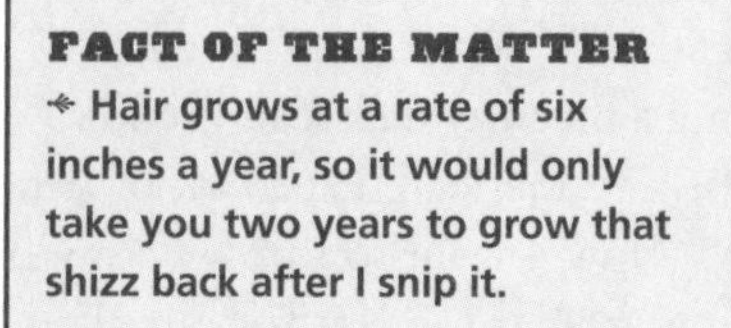

FACT OF THE MATTER

➝ Hair grows at a rate of six inches a year, so it would only take you two years to grow that shizz back after I snip it.

Trust me—trust anyone other than your misguided, insecure sense of style—and chop that napeworm off. You will look hip, not hippie, as though you exist on this side of the Millennium. And if you don't tame the beast, I might not be so kind next time I happen upon you.

PAJAMAS AS OUTERWEAR

PUNCH RATING 👊👊👊👊👊

While I'd like to think of life as one big pillow fight, it's not. It's not a slumber party, and the frozen food section is not Maria Greene's basement, as much as I sometimes wish it were. So why are you wearing pajamas and slippers as you're reaching for those Totino's Pizza Rolls? Put them back and put some clothes on. I think you can find some in Aisle 10.

Dressing has become more and more casual as we slip on flip flops and pull on fleece hoodies for all sorts of occasions. But nightgowns, flannel PJs, and bathrobes cross the Casual Friday line and step into the territory of the crazy, depressed, or those coping with any other state of mind that might demand medication or, at the very least, light therapy.

Admit it: You've thrown in the towel. You might as well just curl up in the fetal position under a Snuggie and give up. I won't kick you while you're down, but do me a favor and keep your crazy behind closed (perhaps locked) doors. If you don't, I'm going to surprise you in the bedding aisle and whack you with a big-ass pillow until you wake the fuck up and change out of your crib clothes.

FACT OF THE MATTER

If you need any sort of cautionary tale about the slippery slope of wearing pajamas outside the house, you only need to look at peopleofwalmart.com.

PARENTS WHO GIVE THEIR OFFSPRING NAMES STARTING WITH THE SAME LETTER

PUNCH RATING

> **FACT OF THE MATTER**
> **↞ These days, the most popular first letter for boys' names is J; for girls' names, it's A. Expectant parents: Back away from the Jacobs and the Avas, please.**

Forget the Octo-Mom; I'm way more disturbed by *19 Kids & Counting*, the TLC show about the Duggar family. Yeah, there are nineteen of them. I could comment about the crazy number of children, but that would be like shooting fish in a barrel. That's not what gripes my ass. Rather, it irritates me when parents give all their kids names starting with the same initial. Jordyn, Jason, Jinger, Jessa, Jill, Joshua, John-David, Jennifer, Jackson, Justin, James—enough already! Would it hurt you to throw a Kevin or Stacey in there, John Jacob Jingleheimer Jackass?

The Duggars aren't alone. I grew up surrounded by kids who came from alliterative households. Carol was kin to Cathy and Christine; Dan's siblings were Dave, Debbie, and Diana. Dumb.

I don't even know where to begin with George Foreman.

(For the record, my brothers are Chris and John, and my step-sibs are Jay, Joe, Paul, Amy, Denise, and Annette, because, obviously, my parents rock.)

PARKING HOGS

PUNCH RATING 👊👊👊👊👊

You know them. Chances are, you also want to punch these selfish fucks in the face (or shatter their windshields with that baseball bat you keep in the trunk for "emergencies"). I'm talking about the asscaps who park their precious car/truck/SUV/crotch rocket/shitbox caboose over several parking spots. I suspect they want to avoid any damage from neighboring car doors. I got news for you and your insurance provider: Splaying your vehicle across several spots is only going to draw attention to it, and not in any kind of good way.

I have the same violent feelings about this parking violation as I do about people who hate to park their car on the street instead of a garage, or are scared to drive it into the big bad city. If you are that worried about your ride, you prolly shouldn't take it out of the cul de sac.

But maybe you have a good reason for flunking your driving test on a daily basis. Perhaps you're visually challenged. Or confused—no, that line in front of you is not a guide for centering your Hummer.

Get your OCD on and make it a challenge NOT to touch either line, instead of straddling it like Tara Reid on a mechanical bull. If you keep it up, I'm going to get jiggy with the parking piggy. I'm going to drive up your insurance premiums when I smash into your beloved Beemer from whatever angle you've provided me with. And if that doesn't do the trick, I'm going to really go Kathy Bates on you and get out the sledgehammer. I'll make sure you're not driving or parking anything but a bicycle anytime soon.

FACT OF THE MATTER

✦ Parking spots are generally seven and a half to nine feet wide. When you have a ginormous SUV muffin topping into my space, it's no surprise that I'm going to ding your paint job with my door.

PATCHOULI

PUNCH RATING

Damn you, patchouli! I cannot stomach your musky stink one minute longer. Much like peach schnapps, a whiff of you makes me throw up a little in my mouth. While this isn't a good thing in any situation, it's especially bad in this case, since I really need to breathe through my mouth to avoid you.

> **FACT OF THE MATTER**
> ✦ In addition to repelling people, patchouli has been used as an insect repellent and even as an antidote to snakebites.

On a recent flight, I was seated next to a couple of old-school hippies. They were ripe. I aimed the vent right at my nose and tried my best to sleep. But my puny olfactory sense was no match for their mighty stench.

What's worse, if I brush against anything with you on it, your funk spams itself all over me and I can't get it off. Can you imagine my nausea-laced mortification when I bumped into someone while doused in patchouli right before an important meeting? I was trying to impress, and I smelled like Haight-Ashbury during a 1969 heat wave.

To those fans of ratchouli, let me just say that dabbing on an overpowering fragrance in lieu of bathing only works for the French. Are you trying to brand yourself as a free spirit? Newsflash, Sunshine Rainbow Quinoa, you're trying to fit in by wearing comfort sandals and reeking of patchoupee, just as much as if you were wearing the latest trend and spritzing yourself with a designer fragrance.

I think a Silkwood-style scrubdown is in order to exfoliate that shit down the drain, followed by a tomato juice bath to neutralize any lingering skunk. Finally, my daisy-fresh friends and I will form a circle around you and pummel you with hacky sacks, while alternately spraying aerosol deodorant and Febreeze in your general direction.

PEACH SCHNAPPS

PUNCH RATING

Setting: Triangle Fraternity, somewhere in Michigan, sometime in the '80s...

Enter a brainy co-ed wearing a peach-colored shirt from Contempo Casuals and that awesome pair of Guess jeans with the zippers at the ankles. You know what I'm talking about.

> **FACT OF THE MATTER**
> **German schnapps is clear with a light fruit flavor. Peach schnapps is something else. An Amercian creation, it is a blend of grain spirits, fruit flavor, sugar, and glycerin, which in combination bring to mind cough syrup.**

Well, the brainiac wasn't so smart that particular night, as she was also packing a pint of peach schnapps. Even though the engineering fraternity usually had an open bar at its parties, it was inconvenient to interrupt a heated game of eight-ball or Twister to get a fresh Fuzzy Navel. So she brought her own, alternately taking swigs and reapplying her frosty Clinique lipstick, the one she got as a gift with purchase.

You know what happened next.

Wildly drunk, she had the walking spins, bent down to pick up something, accidentally got kneed in the eye, yacked, and finally passed out after Maria or someone got her back to South Quad.

The next day was not pretty, and not only because of her black eye.

To this day, the less-than-brainy graduate can suss out that treacly syrup in any punch. Just a soupçon of that smell brings on da acid reflux. To add insult to my injury, it doesn't smell or taste remotely like the real thing. Peach schnapps gives peaches a bad rap. It's time to punch the evil that is peach schnapps in the schnoz. Better yet, I'm going to pour it into a vat near Fraternity Row, set it on fire, and let co-eds get that warm, fuzzy feeling without the threat of puking.

PENIS NAMES

PUNCH RATING

Big Daddy, Cock Hudson, Unihorn, Richard Dixon, Carl, One-Eyed Willie, Casanova, Sir Lancelot, Ralph.

You see where I'm going with this. If you're a dude, chances are good that you've dubbed your dick.

Ever since I read *Forever...* by Judy Blume in junior high, I've been aware that guys have a penchant for naming their junk. I can appreciate the package as much as the next girl. I just don't need to be on a first-name basis with it.

I've got a few names for your Johnson, Junior, and none of them are found in the Big Book of Baby Names. Your little Richard doesn't have a birth certificate, it doesn't have a separate heartbeat, and it doesn't merit a name. While my lady bits are remarkable, I'm not christening them and requesting a Social Security number. They are much loved, yet remain nameless.

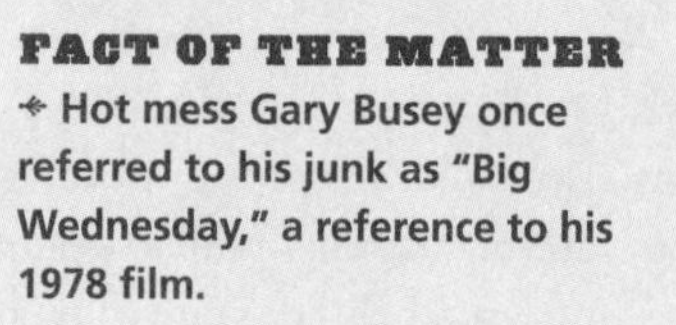
FACT OF THE MATTER

✦ Hot mess Gary Busey once referred to his junk as "Big Wednesday," a reference to his 1978 film.

Your constant cumpanion needs to be put in its place, namely your drawers. And I know just the thing to turn Voldemort's Wand into He Who Shall Not Be Named.

Say hello to my little friend. Its name is Left Fist and it's ready to, uh, whack these upstarts into global amnesia anonymity. A penis by any other name would sound as beat.

PEOPLE WHO BLAB ON RED-EYES

PUNCH RATING 👊👊

You've made your connection, and he's in the aisle seat. It's like some sort of dreamy Sofia Coppola movie, and you're the romantic lead. You're enjoying pillow talk with a sexy stranger who may be your true love, or at least your ticket into the Mile High Club. Sorry to interrupt, but can you do me a favor?

Shut. The. Fuck. Up.

I don't care what time zone we are currently flying over—my internal clock and my wristwatch say it's 3:30 in the morning. I took this flight and an Ambien because I'm good at sleeping on planes. I have my rituals: I don't drink caffeine, I listen to Joni Mitchell laced with Sufjan Stevens, and I wrap myself in my giant knitted shawl.

All I ask is that a bratty toddler not kick my seat and that you Shut. The. Fuck. Up.

> **FACT OF THE MATTER**
> ✦ **In the 2005 film *Red Eye*, poor Rachel McAdams makes the mistake of talking with a sexy stranger, who turns out to be a terrorist planning an assassination. Moral of the story: Never talk on a red-eye.**

Even with headphones on, I can hear you yammering away with your life story and relationship history (which, from the sound of it, you might want to keep to yourself until the third date; just a thought).

When I ask if you could lower your voice because every other single person on the plane is trying to sleep (as evidenced by the pitch-black cabin and profusion of navy blankets, sleep masks, and earbuds), you stare at me as if I just killed your dog. I explain that of course you have the right to talk, but that I'm just asking for some courtesy toward your fellow travelers. Bring the volume down or I'm going to descend into madness and punch you in the face. Forget about true love's kiss from Prince Charming in 18C. Your kiss is on my fist when they turn out the lights.

PEOPLE WHO DON'T BELIEVE IN TV

PUNCH RATING

I've been on loads of first dates that proved to be the last date as well. None of these guys were sociopaths or suffering from acute halitosis. Oh sure, some were inconsiderate and some were cheap, but none of them were bad guys per se (the bad boys usually get a second date).

> **FACT OF THE MATTER**
> **In his book, *Everything Bad Is Good for You,* Stephen Johnson makes the case for watching TV. When it comes to television, even a turd of a reality show, Johnson argues that it's not the content that matters, but the cognitive work your mind is doing while staring at Snooki's cooch.**

No, my biggest beef with many of my dates was that they didn't own a television.

They weren't moving cross-country or suffering from a broken plasma screen. It may seem inconceivable, but there are folks in the world who don't believe in TV.

Bend over and take a deep breath. It helps the dizziness.

I watch more than my share of TV. *America's Next Top Model* is not for everyone, I grant you. But for me, being on the pop culture superhighway is part of what defines me, as well as what educates and entertains me. Watching TV provides me with conversational currency. What in the world do these pretentious fucks have to talk about? Seriously?

Without a TV, flat-screen or otherwise, how can you stay apprised of Tyra's latest tutorials? Or get unexpectedly sucked into a Ken Burns documentary or Shark Week? Or bear witness to the majesty of a royal wedding or the maid of honor's ass?

You can't.

I'm not talking about the high-tech nerd who streams stuff on his laptop or catches the latest episode of *Dr. Who* on an iPhone. No, he's exempt from my rage. He isn't throwing the baby out with the RGB bathwater. I'm talking about the cappuccino intellectual who stuffs a tattered copy of Proust into an NPR tote bag while listening to Philip Glass and sporting a fedora.

In other words, a massive tool.

PEOPLE WHO STOP AT THE TOP OF ESCALATORS

PUNCH RATING

Um, excuse me. You there at the top of the escalator. No, not you. That guy. The completely unaware yambag checking his watch, looking at a map, looking anywhere but behind him. EXCUSE ME! I'm about to rear-end you, and not in a good way. Where the fuck do you think I and the rest of moving humanity queued up behind you are going to go?

> **FACT OF THE MATTER**
> The first working escalator was built alongside a pier at Coney Island in 1896. You'd think people would have learned how to use them by now.

Up your ass, that's where. Escalators don't break for boobs, Einstein, and neither does my ire. I'm going to create my own moving walkway and I'm going to call it "Your Back." Are you listening now?

PEOPLE WHO WATCH ALL THE MOVIE CREDITS

PUNCH RATING

The movie's over. I know this because I hear the strains of some shitbox Celine song and I see credits rolling.

This is my cue to vamanos. I just saw *Scream* 2. The theater's still dark. I could get cut if I stay in my seat popping Milk Duds. Anyway, I have to hit the head. It was a 90-minute movie, after all.

There's just one problem. Gene Shalit next to me is gazing at the screen as though it's the beginning of *Star Wars*.

Excuse me, sir, did you work on the film? Are you in the business? Did you happen to be in Utah for Sundance last year? Is Zach Galifianakis your second cousin? Do you think there's a clue to an episode of *Lost* embedded somewhere between the grip and best boy credits? Do you sleep with your eyes open? No? Then why are you still sitting there? You're blocking my passage, and the ushers need to clean up the remnants of your jumbo combo snack box before the next screening.

Sure, if outtakes or additional footage are part of the credits, I'm right there with you. I don't want to miss Will Ferrell's ad-libbing hilarity either. But that's not usually the case. If you have to watch the credits because you're avoiding going home to an empty or angry house or because you're an aficionado who says "film" instead of "movie" and takes your two-week vacation during your city's film festival, at least have the decency to sit in the middle of a row so I don't have to play impromptu aisle Twister. Consider doing what any self-respecting film buff does: study IMDB when you get home.

FACT OF THE MATTER

The closing credits for the extended edition of *The Lord of the Rings: The Return of the King* clocks in at just under ten minutes, ample time to claw off your own face.

If I have to give you one more lap dance as I'm exiting stage right, I'm going to pack a boom mic in my bag along with my contraband snacks and go Darth Maul on you.

PETTING ZOOS

PUNCH RATING

Petting zoos chap my hide. Ever since I was a kid field tripping to Deer Forest and buying a cone of food pellets from a vending machine, I have been skeeved out by the sad congregation of random critters bleeting out a lethargic greeting.

Or maybe that llama is just pleading with me to put it out of its misery.

It may not be surrounded by water, but a petting zoo is an island of misfit farm animals. Sure, I'm a regular girl who lives for pony rides, but my dream doesn't involve a bony nag tied to a creaking equestrian merry-go-round. I love deer…when they are happily springing away from me in the forest. I find sheep adorbs, but I don't want to pet their fleece; I want to knit it. I'm interested in the cheese—not the E. coli—that a molting goat is offering up.

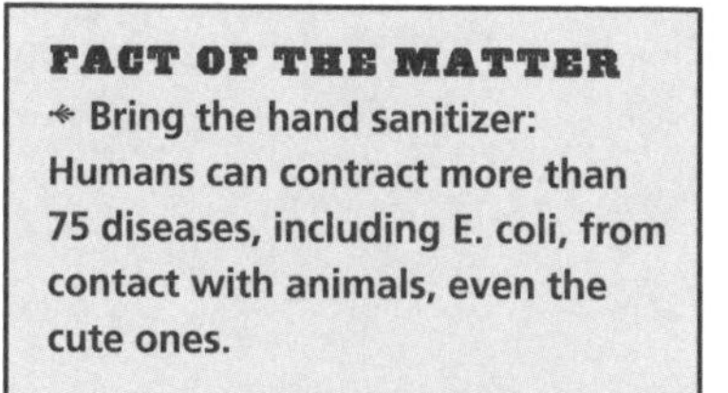

FACT OF THE MATTER

✦ Bring the hand sanitizer: Humans can contract more than 75 diseases, including E. coli, from contact with animals, even the cute ones.

The poo zoo review is in: This one's a stinker.

POLLEN

PUNCH RATING

> **FACT OF THE MATTER**
> ✦ **Ragweed is the biggest offender of hay fever, which affects ten to twenty percent of Americans. And that's nothing to sniff at.**

I know plants need you to grow and shit, but do you have to rub it in our faces (especially my right eye, which is almost swollen shut because of your need to be front and center)? I swear, you're just like a Kardashian: If we stop talking about you for a minute, you have to whip up a new kontroversy to get karried along in the wind. Get over yourself and let something else shine for once. Have you ever considered that mold spores might like a moment now and again?

I don't mean to be a major ragweed, but enough is enough. I'm tired—seriously, I need a nap—of breathing only through my mouth. It's time to make hay, not hay fever, while the sun shines, which means I need to wash you and your allergen pals outta my hair, off of my skin, and down the drain. I'm going to drown your greedy sinus-squatting ass in vats of antihistamines and decongestants. Maybe that'll teach you to keep to your turf and fertilize flora, not my nasal passages…microscopic bitch.

PRECIOUS MOMENTS

PUNCH RATING

These china clowns, cherubs, and rascals skipped through the nightmares of my youth, and I'm still holding a grudge (when I'm not huddled in the fetal position). They traveled in big-eyed packs, alongside Love's Baby Soft, window crystals, and rainbow stickers. They may have been pastel, but they were far from soothing.

Precious Moments really exploded when I was knee-sock-deep into Catholic school, so it was no surprise that I was initially drawn to their cheeky innocence. I had one particularly adorbs lamb that I lifted from a nativity scene. I wanted to hug it and kiss it and call it my own. After about five minutes, however, I moved onto Shaun Cassidy and put my porcelain pet out to pasture.

But that was not enough to corral the horror. Tears of a clown would rain down my face at the thought of the baby mimes and toddler princesses littering the Hallmark store at the local strip mall. What really gets my goat now is the thought of all these evil Enesco eyesores sitting on shelves and in cabinets around the world. I'll finally give them an actual reason for those sad eyes: my hammer coming toward their shiny, happy faces.

FACT OF THE MATTER

For fans wanting to make a pilgrimage, the Precious Moments Chapel can be found in all its wide-eyed glory in Carthage, Missouri.

PROLIFIC DEAD PEOPLE

PUNCH RATING

I see dead people...everywhere.

As if I didn't already have enough self-loathing, dead people are churning out more stuff than I am. Tupac seems to have a new album of unreleased tracks dropping every other year. Michael Jackson had barely settled into his cryogenic chamber before the output kicked in. Jeff Buckley and Stieg Larsson didn't cash in until they checked out. Like another day at the office, the late David Foster Wallace posthumously published another book that none of us will be smart enough to understand. In a creepy turn of events, Nat King Cole duetted with his daughter Natalie from beyond the grave, even managing to join her during a live performance. They may have flatlined, but the status quo seems curiously unchanged.

> **FACT OF THE MATTER**
> **Tupac Shakur has released seven posthumous studio albums. This does not include the live (ironic, *n'est pas*?), remix, and soundtrack albums, not to mention his recent "live" performance at Coachella.**

I think I'm a pretty useful member of society. I knock out words, articles, blogs, books. I create. But I'm a sad-ass somnambulant snail compared with these pulseless workaholics. Why do I even try when I'm getting lapped by corpses? Please folks, give it a rest.

QUADRABOOB & UNIBOOB

PUNCH RATING

Any sort of ill-fitting bra on myself or anyone else chaps my hide (particularly around my chest). Just like jeans that are too small, the wrong fit will give you a muffin top up top—not a tasty look.

Quadraboob looks terrible and feels even worse. Are two breasts not enough for you? Do you need to one-up (or two-up) the rest of us by stuffing yourself into a cup size so small that your bodacious boobies spill up and over, clearly trying to escape their Lycra vise? Like wishing for unicorns or Edward Cullen, telling yourself that you're a 34C doesn't bring it into being.

> **FACT OF THE MATTER**
> **It's not rocket science: Circumference of torso over the fullest part of your tits minus the circumference of torso directly under the breast = cup size (1 inch per cup; e.g. 3 inches = C cup)**

Then there's the uniboob, which, if you haven't had this mammary treat thrown in your face, occurs when you stuff your junk into a tight bra bandage so that you get one lump sum across your chest. Sure, the girls will be immobilized during a workout, but this ta-ta tube will also look like you're squirreling away a loaf of bread or a salami in your shirt. While delicious, they sure can't compare with your luscious décolletage.

Beeline to your nearest lingerie department and get fitted. Yes, you may be a size larger than you thought, but if you keep smothering and smashing and shoving your breasts into a compression bandage, I'm going to have to fill an over-the-shoulder boulder holder with an actual boulder and knock some sense into you.

RENAISSANCE FAIRES

PUNCH RATING

As the weather warms up, my thoughts naturally turn to sunscreen, outdoor cinema, beach vacations...and, unfortunately, Renaissance Faires. From meadow to wood, these traveling minstrel shows set up shoppe for a few days of costumed frivolity. Celebrating the age of the Bard, RenFaires provide a balm to the spirit, a respite from the modern storm, a step back in time, a rare opportunity to rub starched linen elbows with the occasional jongleur....

In other words, these most rare and precious of gatherings are a time to inflict some serious old-school torture.

Ye Olde Newsflashe: If you're carrying a lute, you clay-witted codpiece, you're gonna get your ass kicked. The Dark Ages may be over but I'm still going to make your world go black. To aid me in my quest, I call upon my noble and true hand puppet. With mini club in hand, Punch can swing away in the direction of your jingly jester hat. With a heavy tankard, he can swipe at wenches and whelps in kind. This is one Renaissance man I can get behind.

Verily.

FACT OF THE MATTER

Most RenFaires are set during the reign of Queen Elizabeth I, the height of the English Renaissance; curiously, few to none are set during the actual Italian Renaissance.

FACT OF THE MATTER

We have the Renaissance Pleasure Faire of Southern California to thank for all the merriment; it's regarded as the first modern RenFaire, opening in 1962.

SCRABBLE

PUNCH RATING

I suck at Scrabble. I mean, I suck dead bear dry. I don't know if I get too caught up in trying to wow everyone with an OED-worthy word. Maybe I'm fixated on the triple-word score. Whatever the case, I get a serious ass-whupping every time, usually by a seventh grader or a great-grandparent.

I want to punch Scrabble and its smug ten-point Z tiles right where it counts—namely those 101 two-letter words—because they are a reminder of how inept I am. I like to avoid humiliation at all costs, so why would I belly up to the coffee table and let my friends and family in on the fact that my English degree was a waste, along with that dictionary I got for my 16th birthday? What good is it knowing big words when I get routinely trounced by xi, qi, and do re mi?

FACT OF THE MATTER

Architect Alfred Mosher Butts (total letter score: twenty-eight) created the game in 1938, figuring out the distribution and points of each letter based on a frequency analysis of letters from such sources as the *New York Times*.

I may not get the triple-letter score, but I do have a five-fingered fist that will produce a five-point word. In a word, OW.

SEAT HOGS

PUNCH RATING

After suffering through planes, trains, and automobiles, I've had it with all the greedy fucks who ooze over several seats. At the airport, businessmen ignore the masses at the jam-packed gate and set up shop with their computer and carry-on to one side, meal to the other, and cords snaking out and plugging up all the available outlets.

On the bus, selfish hosebeasts sit on the aisle, cock blocking the empty window seat next to them by dumping a backpack on it, or simply ignoring my presence behind sun-blocking shades or pretending to be asleep.

Move your fat faker ass, and your little dog too!

If you insist on being a waste of space, I'm afraid I have no choice but to assume the seat of power and hand your ass to you on a silver platter. You'll feel the earth move under your feet as I herd you to a standing-room-only area for the duration of your trip. If you covet your neighbor's seat again, I'm going to gather up your belongings, pile them in your lap, and wrap you in yellow "POLICE—DO NOT CROSS" tape. That should contain you nicely while I punch your greedy gob. Awake now? No? Then you won't feel it when I smother you with your travel pillow.

FACT OF THE MATTER

Gordon Gekko famously said, "Greed, for lack of a better word, is good." And you see how well that worked out for him. So pick up your ratty messenger bag and move yo' greedy ass.

SHOELESS HOUSEHOLDS

PUNCH RATING

Increasingly, when I enter someone's home, I'm shoehorned into a foyer lined with shoes and instructed to add mine to the pile.

Um, I came for a party, not for a pedicure.

I get that folks don't want their hardwoods scratched and scuffed by my stilettos. I understand that paranoid parents are afraid of the germs that I'm tracking in on the soles of my shoes.

Call me a heel, but I don't want to walk around in my socks or bare feet. My shoes deserve to be seen as God and Christian Louboutin intended: on my feet. And without the boost of the heel I am never without, my jeans sweep the floor. From my POV, this has only one bright side: My friends' floors never need to be mopped. My pant legs and socks do it for them.

FACT OF THE MATTER

According to the Janka Ball Rating system, Brazilian Cherry is the hardest wood for flooring, so fork over the extra cash for your hardwood floors and let guests keep their shoes on.

If people keep demanding that I kick off rather than kick up my heels, I am going to kick them in the face—right after I shuffle around their house with 80-grit sandpaper taped to my feet.

SIDEWALK HOGS

PUNCH RATING

When people ask me if I'd rather have the superpower of invisibility or flight, I always go with flight.

Apparently, I'm already invisible.

At least it seems that way when I'm strolling through my neighborhood and spy two or three chuckleheads walking toward me. Talking to each other, they don't give up an INCH of space. They don't acknowledge my existence. They wouldn't know if I was tricked out in fetish gear or pointing a flamethrower directly at them. As these fuckers approach, it becomes a game of sidewalk chicken, and I always lose. At the last minute, I veer out of their way, usually tripping into a tree bed or slamming into a building.

No, excuse *me*.

Far be it from me to interrupt, disturb, or derail you, you self-absorbed dickwads with crapass peripheral vision.

> **FACT OF THE MATTER**
> **The average width of a sidewalk is six feet, plenty of room for you and your friend or stroller to let me pass, so move yo' ass.**

Let's not forget about the strollers. I frequently dodge mommies and strollers who greedily spread out across any available paved surface. Believe me, I understand that these gals need to get some sun and girl talk. But let me tell you, they are tough mamas. Infantry units can use these chicks on their front lines, as they never break formation. I can practically see the tumbleweeds as I stare down a fence of Bugaboos and estrogen at high noon. Of course, I wind up looking like a total dick when I try to break on through to the other side.

It's time to take action! I'm staging a silent protest, and I'm asking you to join me. When you encounter a line of people coming at you, stop. Stand still. Break their synchronized stride and make them flow around you. You can pick up the pace after these wastes of space walk on by. If they bump into you, well, I think you know what to do. You saw *The Karate Kid*.

Sweep the leg.

SILK FLOWERS

PUNCH RATING 👊👊👊

Mom, commenting on the décor of the trailer she bought in Texas for the winter months: "My goll, you should have seen this place when we bought it. It was filled with rag-nasty plastic flowers."

Me: "Ugh, I hate those. I mean, what's the point?"

Mom: "Yeah, I threw them out and replaced them with some really nice silk flowers."

Me: "Uh...."

I love that my mother sees a marked class difference between plastic and silk flowers. To me, they are all the same: fake, non-fragranced doodads I have to dust. Why clutter up your home with bouquets of immortal meh?

I realize you may not be home long enough to keep a plant alive or you have a black thumb or you can't afford to buy cut flowers very often or your cat could die if he chewed on a lily, but here's my question: Why do you need anything at all? If you like the look of flowers, just get a print of some sunflowers or put a daisy magnet on the fridge. Don't clutter up the place with phony ferns and bogus pots of orchids.

> **FACT OF THE MATTER**
> **Most fake flowers on the market are not silk—they're polyester. Whatever the case, rest happy in the knowledge that both types are treated to be flame retardant.**

Nip these faux-ers in the bud and leave them where they belong: in a retail garden (i.e., Michaels, aisle 7).

SKYMALL

PUNCH RATING

Three hours into a flight from hell, a Meerkat Gang Sculpture is starting to look pretty damn good. In fact, I don't know how I ever lived without it. What's happening to me? Who am I?

The trip starts out okay: I've taken my Dramamine and I've got snacklets, an aisle seat, plenty of reading material, my laptop, and some sort of craft project.

Then it all goes to shit.

The seats are too small to pull out my laptop or knit, let alone stretch my legs. The guy next to me smells like 1969 and the overhead vent is not assuaging the stench. The 3-year-old behind me is taking great delight in kicking my seatback while crying without pause. I plow through my rag mags in short order. Clearly, there's nothing left to live for…so I pull out the SkyMall catalog.

When, at 30,000 feet, I think I've hit rock bottom, things gets worse. I feel very 1993 by way of Franklin Covey as I contemplate a framed print of a Zen garden. Ooh, where do I swipe my card? Oh wait, here's a light therapy system! For only $399.95, I can make my frown turn upside down in my rainy hometown! A plantar fasciitis kit? Now you're just freakin' my shit out, SkyMaul—you're reaching into my soul and uncovering my deepest desires. In fact, I think I just might….Holy fuck, a watch winder! If only there was an automatic piehole feeder and a bum wiper, I could just throw in the towel.

Before I give up on life and go down the battery-operated rabbit hole, I need to do one last thing: unleash a can of whoop ass on this twisted love child of QVC and Lillian Vernon. A few repurposed items should do the trick.

I don a Doolittle & Loafmore sweatshirt and LED-lighted safety glasses and get to business. I collect a plane's worth of DieMall catalogs in an NFL hammock. I heap them into a copper fire pit and crumple up a wall-size crossword puzzle as tinder. With my Swarovski lighter, I torch the hot mess. No number of indoor hoses and plant waterers can help you now. Go back from whence you came, demon catalog, and take Hammacher Schlemmer and its schtupid name with you.

FACT OF THE MATTER

Founded in 1990, SkyMall now reaches 650 million air travelers each year. Along with nose-hair trimmers, the Mosquito Magnet, a device that attracts and kills mosquitoes, is one of the catalog's all-time best sellers.

SPINNING BEACH BALL

PUNCH RATING

My computer is on its last legs, I get it. I don't have to hear the death rattle to know its days are numbered. But yet my MacBook has to keep reminding me that it's a hunk o' junk. In fact, it throws it in my face in the form of an obnoxious beach ball that frolics all over my screen, mocking me and my three-year-old equipment.

> **FACT OF THE MATTER**
> **Before Apple's "spinning wait ball," there was a wristwatch that appeared on the screen when everything else froze on the screen. It was equally aggravating.**

Apparently, my rotten Apple can't keep Word from quitting on me but it can still muster up the energy to flip me the rainbow bird.

I hate to wait to begin with. Throw the spinning Trivial Pursuit pie into the mix and you have a serious suck cocktail. Since baby needs to write, I have to resist the urge to punch my laptop in its smug but increasingly ineffective LCD face. But on the rainbow brite side, while I wait for the beach ball to get its yayas out, I have ample time to think about how I'm going to burst this trouble bubble when I finally upgrade.

STAYCATIONS

PUNCH RATING

This has been the era of the "staycation," a dumbass euphemism for being too broke to go anywhere interesting. Instead, people are encouraged to discover their own town, to go on holiday in their own backyard—literally, their own backyard. Instead of flying to a foreign country, renting a condo at the beach, or roadtripping to Branson, set up a tent on your patio and sleep al fresco. What could be better?

Um, most anything.

If you are sitting on your couch for two weeks, you're not on vacation. You're unemployed or broke or both. Vacationing at home only makes you think about the shit you have to get done. Instead of recharging your batteries on this naycation, you'll paint the kitchen, record your expenses into Quicken, grout the tub. Some holiday. It almost beats that time when you were 11 and you went on that last cross-country family roadtrip before your parents split up, doesn't it?

> **FACT OF THE MATTER**
> "Staycation" was added to Merriam-Webster's Collegiate Dictionary in 2009, proving once again that the Oxford English Dictionary is the way to go.

Naming it something annoyingly cute doesn't make it so. Just look at Soleil Moon Frye or the critter from Gremlins. Yeah, Gizmo was darling…until you added water. A staycation sounds appealing…until you realize that you just reorganized your closet, waxed the floors as well as your bits and pieces, and sewed all the missing buttons on your clothing. Productive? Yes. Relaxing? Just stay no.

Don't even get me going about babymoons….

STEAMPUNK

PUNCH RATING

I like imagination. I like creativity. I don't like this Victorian goth take on the Renaissance Faire. Instead of a jongleur in a jester's cap, steampunkers strap on leather goggles and embrace a good Rube Goldberg machine or Tesla coil for shits and giggles.

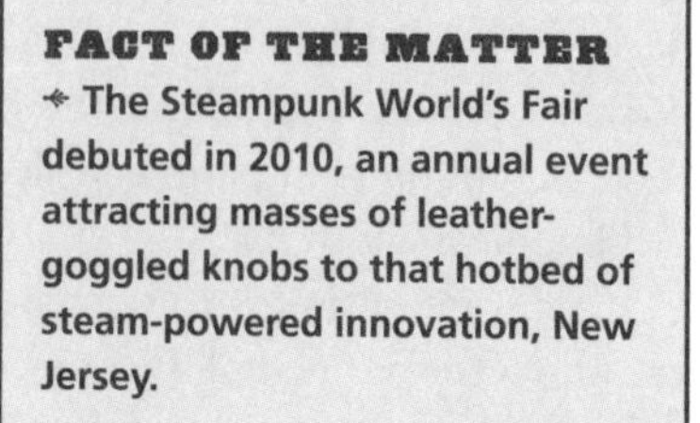

FACT OF THE MATTER

✦ The Steampunk World's Fair debuted in 2010, an annual event attracting masses of leather-goggled knobs to that hotbed of steam-powered innovation, New Jersey.

The thing is, as Billy Joel would say, the good old days weren't always good. If you're going to fire up some steam-powered contraptions using your erector set, you'd best showcase the tuberculosis and smallpox that rocked 19th-century Britain as well.

You aren't edgy or alternative. You're just a former LOTR/Star Wars/D&D fan dressed up as an H.G. Wells wet dream. Doff the leather waistcoat and travel back to the present before I engage in a little time travel of my own and sic a Morlock on you.

STRIPPER BROWS

PUNCH RATING 👊👊👊👊

I really have to draw the line. Pencil-thin brows and sperm brows don't belong on the face. Put those sad things in a sterile cup where they belong.

I admit it: I plucked the fuck out of my eyebrows in seventh grade in an unfortunate experiment during a boring weekend. It was around the same time that I tried cutting my own bangs. Add to that a bad perm and you've got a whole lot of not-pretty going on. I tried to take some artsy shots, and since they were a bit out of focus, I looked a bit like Marlene Dietrich. Oh, who am I kidding? I looked like nine miles of bad road.

I digress.

Over the past couple of years, I've been letting the brows grow in while simultaneously watching a whole lot of reality TV. Invariably the skank shows are riddled with crippled eyebrows. Some are drawn on in a thin line (see Pam Anderson or John Waters' mustache).

Then there are the cock-tweezers trying to rock sperm brows. You know the kind: They start out sort of full and then they quickly taper to a thin tadpole tail. Is this an announcement that their hoo-hah is open for business? And if the sperm shape isn't bad enough, the over-plucked brows often start somewhere over the pupil instead of the inside corner of the eye, so these dumbasses already look punched in the face and vaguely surprised.

What's the deal? Are these brow-challenged chicks OCD and can't leave them alone? Do they have trichotillomania, working out their issues by pulling out their brows? Are they a living tribute to the comma?

Rather than punching these douchettes in their already damaged faces, I think a bit of hot wax is in order. Avoiding the eyebrow area, I think I'm going to treat you to a full facial wax, since you clearly like depilation so fucking much. And FYI, the standard tip for services rendered is fifteen to twenty percent.

FACT OF THE MATTER

✦ Beware the overplucking! If you ever decide to embrace your inner Brooke Shields, you might be out of pluck. Excessive plucking or waxing can make the hair follicle smaller or even damaged, meaning they may grow back smaller, finer, or not at all.

SUNGLASSES AT NIGHT

PUNCH RATING

Is your future so bright that you've gotta wear shades? Newsflash, Corey Hart, you don't look cool. In fact, can you look at all?

Are you almost famous? Are you Bono? Jack Nicholson at the Oscars? No? Then take those goddamn *Top Gun* aviators off. It's not 1986 and you're not Iceman. Even pilots take their sunglasses off after dark. If you don't remove them, I'm going to take your breath away…literally. My fist feels the need, the need to speed toward your face.

> **FACT OF THE MATTER**
> **In a meta sort of twist, Corey Hart's "Sunglasses at Night" was sampled in the Gym Class Heroes' song, "Blinded by the Sun."**

Can you even make your way through a trendy nightclub when wearing your Oliver Peoples or your BluBlockers? I suppose they could be special superspy glasses that give you night vision or crazy tracking abilities.

But I suspect not.

More likely, they are a fashion crutch intended to lend you an air of L.A. hipness. Allow me to shed some light on the Situation—you don't look cool, you look like a tool in a graphic tee wearing too much hair product. Since you seem to enjoy low lighting, let me do you a favor and make it a permanent condition by blinding you with the bow of your Ray-Bans. Harsh, yes, but so is the cold light of day on your delicate eyes.

TALKING ABOUT ONESELF IN THE THIRD PERSON

PUNCH RATING

"I'm bored of Bono and I am him—I'm sick of me. I felt it was a little limiting to be in the first person," Bono once said. I'm sad that I'm limited in the ways that I can punch him in his pompous face.

My shit is royally irked when someone starts talking about him or herself in the third person. Politicians like Bob Dole and Joe Biden and athletes like Shaq and the Rock have been serving up illeisms for a long time. Yeah, I can smell what the Rock is cooking and it smells like dumbass, with a side of hubris. Are you royalty? A dead celebrity?

> **FACT OF THE MATTER**
> **"Illeism" is the act of talking about yourself in the third person. By the transitive property, it is also the act of being a massive tool.**

I think the only people allowed to refer to themselves in the third person are Steven Hawking, Mr. T, and the Hulk. And oh yeah, Jesus, Buddha, and their pals. That's it, and even then they are walking a fine line between acceptable and my fist. I have found what I'm looking for, Bono, and it's your face.

TENNIS BRACELETS

PUNCH RATING

Forgive my lack of sophisdickation, but does anyone actually play tennis while wearing these? In my mind, jewelry + exercise = silly. Diamond bracelets shouldn't have anything to do with tennis. Like chicklets in Juicy sweatsuits, gals wearing tennis bracelets are most likely not mid-exercise.

The jewelry equivalent of a French manicure, tennis bracelets are nouveau riche. As soulless as Ryan Seacrest, these bourgeoisie baubles don't denote your status on the social ladder; they tag you as sheep. They aren't bracelets as much as leashes. Baby, you may own a few carats of J-grade diamonds, but your ass is metaphorically owned by Kay Jewelers and the Cheesecake Factory.

Since you put the ass in class, I'm going to carve "classy" into your butt cheeks with one of your diamonds. Too harsh? Okay, fine. I'll rip that double fault of wretched excess off your tanorexic wrist and lash you with it instead. I'm just helping you leave your mark.

FACT OF THE MATTER

Chris Evert inadvertently gave these braceletdowns their name when her bracelet broke during a 1987 U.S. Open match. Well played, Chrissie. Well played.

TOPPING OFF COFFEE WITHOUT ASKING

PUNCH RATING 👊👊👊👊

I may be at my favorite watering hole, but I don't want to be watered. I just want to wilt into my chair and relax with a cuppa joe. Everything's coming up roses—until a constant gardener comes out of nowhere and tops off my mug with fresh coffee.

I spring to life.

I had just, finally, after much trial and error, gotten my decaf to the right temperature and the perfect hybrid of cream and sugar. When my guard is down (i.e., I'm eyeballing the hunky chef), regular joe splashes down into my cup, turning it back into the color of dirt.

> **FACT OF THE MATTER**
> **Caffeine can trigger GI issues, and it gives me gas, not what I'm going for in public, so please back away from my coffee cup.**

Color me irked. I know you're trying to be proactive, but you're presumptive. No, I don't need any more coffee. Nope, I don't need it at a boil. Besides, you aproned Einstein, I was drinking decaf, not regular. Here's a tip: Ask me what I want. I just might warm up to you. Continue to go rogue and I'll just have to plant my fist in your face and stunt your growth.

TWENTY-MINUTE COFFEE PREP

PUNCH RATING

I don't know what's going on back there, but this isn't the Manhattan Project. It's a flippin' cup of coffee. While your coffee contraption looks like it was made by Skynet, I'm pretty sure it's not going to enable time travel. And it sure as hell isn't going to help me get back the twenty minutes I've been waiting patiently by the sugar station. What it—and you—are doing, however, is terminating my patience.

You don't need to take the scenic route to get to my drink destination. Really. Just jump on the espressoway and knock that shit out. Don't wax rhapsodic about your special blend that was picked by monkeys on the north face of a mountain in Colombia. Don't spam me with your disdain for my decaf order. And while I appreciate your java jive, I don't need or want you to craft a flower or devil or my silhouette in my cappuccino's microfroth.

> **FACT OF THE MATTER**
> **The first espresso machine was patented in 1884 by Angelo Moriondo. I bet his patent arrived sooner than my latte order.**

And when you take that long, you're setting up unreasonable expectations. If I don't have an orgasm on my first foamy sip, your fine art of grinding, steaming, and frothing is lost on me. And that's truly a shame.

TYPING E-MAILS IN ALL CAPS

PUNCH RATING

When you rip off an e-mail to me using only capital letters, I reckon that you're pissed, lazy, or both. You're pretty much passive-aggressively shouting at me. I'm certainly screaming inside my head reading your rant.

STOP IT.

I'M NOT KIDDING.

I'm a big believer in proper grammar and punctuation, and I feel there's a perfect word or phrase to express every thought or feeling. You don't need to resort to all caps to get your point across. I GET IT!

I also get that you're a monster A-hole who's in serious need of an etiquette class. I don't care that you're rushed, I don't want to hear that your pinkies can't operate the shift key properly, and I really don't give a shit that your hide is chapped. If you want to communicate with me, I'd better see some ascenders and descenders coming at me through my inbox. If there's no x-height to be found, you can bet money that I'm going to seriously font you up and put a cap in your ass, where it belongs.

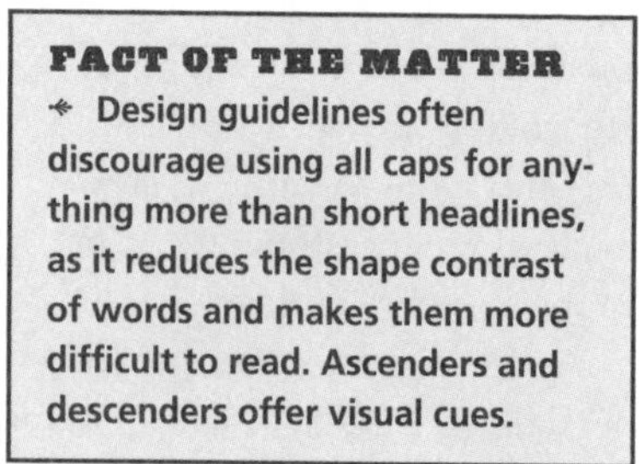
FACT OF THE MATTER

Design guidelines often discourage using all caps for anything more than short headlines, as it reduces the shape contrast of words and makes them more difficult to read. Ascenders and descenders offer visual cues.

UTILIKILTS

PUNCH RATING

Is a Tolkien convention in town, or are the Highland Games looming? Sorry to be a Utilipill, but Jesus, Mary, and Joseph, these man-skirts are fecking dumb. Unless you're heading to a Gathering in your clan's tartan, back away from the Utilikilt. Scotsman Alan Cumming can pull off a kilt when hanging at a gay bar or anywhere else. Gerald Butler can sure as hell make it work. You can't.

> **FACT OF THE MATTER**
> ✦ **Utilikilts have only been around since 2000; the first one was created from a pair of military pants so the founder could tinker with his motorcycle more comfortably (i.e. ventilate his junk).**

What's that, you say? You're hot? Wear some cargo shorts. Edgy? Get a tat. *Lord of the Rings* fan? Move back to the shire, or at least New Zealand. Need a place to stick your tools? I can suggest a few alternatives.

If you insist on never giving up your freedom, I'm going to give you some serious Maclovin'. I'll wrap my arms around your waist and reach for your big tool—namely, your ball-peen hammer. Cue the bagpipes, MacDeath, and get ready for a *Braveheart*-worthy beatdown. And if you persist in your questionable fashion choices, I'll have no choice but to pull out a dirk and go for the Utilikill.

And no, I don't want to see what you've got going on under there.

VANITY PLATES

PUNCH RATING 👊👊👊👊👊

Personalized license plates are NOTSOGR8 in my book. In fact, IH8EM. The vehicular equivalent of the tattoo, they ask you to figure out what sort of six- or eight-letter phrase you're going to slap on your SUV's ass to define yourself. *Seinfeld*'s ASSMAN is ASSIN9, in my humble opinion. A lot of the plates are pretentious and blowhardian in nature (0-60IN4 or WISHURME), some—clearly owned by Stifler's peeps—are downright grody (8 ER OUT? Really, Illinois? Really?). There's a ginormous motor home sporting "GLBL WMR" which should really say "I M PRBLM." Some unoriginal chuckleheads are using online acronyms—if you are ROTFL, who's driving the car? I'm not rolling on the floor, dude. I'm right behind you, willing myself not to rear-end your metal tramp stamp.

My friends in Delaware will pay upwards of five figures for a rare black low-numbered plate. They view it as an investment and a status symbol. This sort of boggles my mind, especially when they tell me how much the single-digit plates go for (the number "6" plate went for $675,000 in 2008). What kind of vehicle deserves to host that sort of marquee plate? Is there a place for it on Air Force 1's vertical stabilizer?

I suppose a vanity plate is a way to show off without shelling out buttloads of clams. There is one plate that I can get behind, both on and off the road. A hearse's plate that reads "U R NEXT." Yep, buddy, you are. Because I M GUNIN 4U.

FACT OF THE MATTER

✦ The Commonwealth of Virginia may be called the "mother of presidents," but it might also be the "mother of jackholes"—it has the highest percentage of vanity plates in the nation.

VENTRILOQUISTS' DUMMIES

PUNCH RATING

Are you looking at me? Ahem, I said, Are. You. Looking. At. Me? Don't just sit there with that insipid smile on your face; answer me, you little twerp!

Silent treatment, huh? Okay, fine. Just sit there and listen. But wipe that smirk off your face before my fist does it for you.

I bet you think it's pretty funny that you give me nightmares. Yeah, it's a freakin' laugh riot. I just love it when you talk to me without moving your lips in that whispery lisp you can't seem to shake. Would it kill you to say words starting with Bs or Ps?

FACT OF THE MATTER

The hardest sounds for ventriloquists to make are f, v, b, p, and m, because one or both of the lips has to move.

Don't look away, you shifty-eyed little spawn of Geppetto. Own your creepy. Lay off the Botox before you morph into Carol Channing (although a little filler like Juvederm would work wonders on those laugh lines; just a thought). Work on your conversational skills and look people in the eye when you're talking to them. And, for the love of Barnum & Bailey, lose the smug mug, you knob, before I turn you into firewood and really light you up.

WHITE CHOCOLATE

PUNCH RATING

Creamy? Yes.
Sugary? Yes.
Waste of space? Hell, yes.
Chocolate? Uh....

I tend to be irritated by things I don't understand. Quantum physics, *Ulysses*, the popularity of Snooki....

So you can imagine my apoplexy when I encounter white chocolate.

Apparently, it's got cocoa butter in it. Big whoop. So does my body lotion, but I'm not going to snack on that either. What it lacks is cocoa paste, liquor, or powder—not to mention cocoa flavor. White chocolate is the confectionery equivalent of *The Hills*. Pointless, flavorless, and mad white.

White chocolate isn't chocolate; it's a crime.

FACT OF THE MATTER

Unlike chocolate that's actually worth eating, white chocolate doesn't contain any antioxidants.

WINDSOCKS

PUNCH RATING

Your windsock stays on my mind. In fact, it's burned into my retina. I've tried to consider the lilies of the field, really I have, but I can't. Because your giant rainbow windsock is spoiling, spinning, and polluting my view.

I already knew you were a Notre Dame fan, thanks to the bumper sticker, license plate frame, and leprechaun antenna ball on your PT Cruiser. I don't need to be reminded of your misguided love, because frankly, I couldn't care less. And like your unfathomable affection for the Fightin' Irish, I also don't give a rat's ass about your penchant for pirates, whales, or snowmen. Why do you feel the need to clog up your yard, porch, stoop, or front door with these garbage bags?

Do you keep your seasonal or themed windsocks in the garage next to the extra lawn gnomes, gazing balls, and inflatable snow globes? Since your windsocks are most likely flame retardant, I think the best way to clean house is to sew these polyester air condoms together, fill them with helium, and create a hot-air balloon that can transport them all back to hell, or at least to the local landfill.

FACT OF THE MATTER

Windsocks are actually used at airports and chemical plants to indicate wind direction and wind speed; I suspect they don't sport flowers or leprechauns.

WINKS

PUNCH RATING

I've dipped my toe into the internet dating waters, and whenever a guy "winks" at me, I go off the deep end. Are you too lazy to write to me? Too busy? Tongue-tied in the face of all of my splendor? Too fucking bad. Grow a pair and send me a real note.

It doesn't need to be an 8,000-word missive (I've gotten one of those). It doesn't need to lay open your soul, telling me how much I remind you of your ex-wife (yep, got that too). It just needs to say hi, be real, and, if you've got an extra five minutes, tell me something about yourself or why you liked my profile.

But whatever you do, don't "wink" at me, you wuss.

Winks make me batshit crazy. To me, they scream, "I care enough to send the very least." Do you think I'm going to be so taken with your snapshot (the one where you've clearly cropped out your last girlfriend or draped your cat artfully over your girth) that I'll go straight to your profile and become inspired to initiate the conversation?

Dream on, Lothari-NO.

"You don't know what you're missing," you say? You're absolutely right. I have absolutely no idea what I'm missing. However, I do know what you're missing: courage and perhaps a time-management system that allows you to spend more than ten seconds contacting a potential love interest. Wink at me again and I'll give you a response. How about, "This person has blocked you from her profile?" Get some game or get lost.

FACT OF THE MATTER

A real wink usually conveys shared secret knowledge with someone. When you wink on a dating site, that secret is, "Hey, guess what? I'm too lame to man up and send you a real e-mail."

XTINA

PUNCH RATING 👊👊

The Voice is glorious. It even managed to make *Burlesque* worth watching (reader: don't judge; that's my job). But for the love of Christ, why did you have to pornify yourself, Triple-Xing your brand by calling yourself Xtina? It chaps my hide, much the way those assless chaps must have chafed when you filmed your Dirrty video.

> **FACT OF THE MATTER**
> **The girl's sold more than 50 million units, making more than enough money to buy a vowel or two.**

While you had a brief foray into retro Andrews Sisters style, you have by and large committed to an xtreme look, with fried platinum extensions, spackled-on makeup, and too-tight clothes originally intended to fit Barbie dolls. What a girl wants is for you to stop dressing like a brittle stripper and put the Christ back in Christina.

If you don't, I'm going to launch my fist toward your face. X marks the spot.

YEAR-ROUND CHRISTMAS DECORATIONS

PUNCH RATING

As we move into spring, we—like Julius Caesar before us—are tipped off to beware the Ides of March. But I think we need to keep an eye out for the real killer: Christmas shit that hasn't been taken down by March.

The holidays are usually a disappointment, so why prolong the agony well into the new year? Do you enjoy jacked-up electric bills? Do you get some sort of sick satisfaction by turning your house into a giant nightlight for your cul de sac? Does the Christmas spirit live within you and your candy-cane cardigan 365 days a year? Are you simply a lazy fuck?

You took down the inflatable snow globe, you say? Shut your effin' elfin trap. You've still got a sleigh parked on the roof and a flocked tree peeking out of the picture window. You might as well stick a red-and-green sign in your front yard that says, "I deserve to get run over by a reindeer."

Whatever the case, let me spell it out: Strands of icicle lights, while I stomach them for a five-week period in November and December, are not mood lighting. Tinsel is not to be trifled with after the first week of January. Send the holiday sweaters packing. And above all, a Christmas tree, real or artificial, is not a houseplant. After the holidays, it's an eyesore.

If you let your figgy pudding freak flag fly year-round, here's how I'm going to join in your celebration. I'm going to repurpose the little drummer boy's snare drum and smash it over your head. I might grind up a little mistletoe and slip it into your eggnog. And if your house looks like Santa's workshop and crocuses are blooming outside, I'm going fill your stocking with lumps of coal and get Kris Kringle on your ass. Ho, ho, ho, motherfucker.

FACT OF THE MATTER

In some civilized places, decorations are taken down on Twelfth Night (January 5th or 6th).

ZUMBA

PUNCH RATING

I want to like you, I really do. But while it seems like a requirement to wear a sports bra and to oil your abs in order to join the dance party, Zumba is the fitness equivalent of mom jeans. With its caliente Latino beats, it signals that you are clapping your way into middle age with abandon.

It might also mean that you miss Jazzercise something fierce.

I get that you want something to give meaning to your fitness life. Ever since your neighborhood Curves closed and your Tae Bo VHS tape snapped, you've been keen to step up your cardio. And since you love shaking it to the Macarena and the Chicken Dance, this seems like a perfect Kinection.

FACT OF THE MATTER

Colombia isn't just the home of Sophia Vergara and Pablo Escobar; Zumba was first conceived in Colombia in the 1990s by Alberto "Beto" Perez.

But you don't need Dumba and your local community center. Rather, pop your Menudo cassette into your Walkman and just dance. That combo never gets old.

AND ONE FINAL SELECTION FOR SHITS AND GIGGLES...

BOOKS DERIVED FROM BLOGS

PUNCH RATING

I'll take this one square in the face. I can get as good as I give, and after punching 101 ridiculous things that this white person doesn't like, I can fess up to my own self-loathing.

Is there anything more maddening than seeing blogs that have managed to make their way onto a publisher's front list and the Urban Outfitters sale table? These jackasses managed to monetize their blog with crap writing, a dumb idea, or user-generated content! Fuck My Life, indeed.

But not all blogbooks are created equal. Some are fucking brilliant. In fact, I wish I'd written them. And therein lies the rub. My jealousy is working on many levels. I'm chapped that these blauthors are better writers. I'm pissed that they figured out how to connect with and attract a massive online audience. I want their fat book advance. In short, I want to go Single White Blogger on them and assume their charmed life, both cyber and otherwise.

FACT OF THE MATTER

Leveraging the popularity of his blog, Christian Lander's *Stuff White People Like* became a *New York Times* best-selling book in 2008. I think of *Things I Want to Punch in the Face* as "Stuff This Particular White Person Doesn't Like."

ABOUT THE AUTHOR

JENNIFER WORICK

is a Seattle-based author of more than twenty books on humor, pop culture, and crafts, including two best-selling *Worst Case Scenario* books (Chronicle) and the hit *Nancy Drew's Guide to Life* (Running Press). She also writes the Things I Want to Punch in the Face blog and another called word., as well as many magazine articles. In her spare time, she puts on seminars about the business of book publishing *and* travels the country to deliver a hilarious slide-show presentation about dating and sex to college students. You can learn more at jenniferworick.com.